TWO CENTS TO SAVE AMERICA

Perry Johnson

Foreword by Dr. Arthur Laffer

PERRY JOHNSON
PUBLISHING

Other Titles by the Author

ISO 9000: Meeting the New International Standards
First edition, McGraw-Hill, Inc., 1973

ISO 9000: Meeting the New International Standards
Second edition, McGraw-Hill Companies, 1993

ISO 9000: The Year 2000 and Beyond
Third Edition, McGraw-Hill Companies, 2000

Keeping Score: Strategies and Tactics for Winning the Quality War
Ballinger Publishing Company, 1989

ISO 14000 Road Map to Registration
McGraw-Hill Companies. 1997

ISO 14000 The Business Manager's Complete Guide to Environmental Management
John Wiley & Sons, 1997

Contents

List of Figures

List of Cartoons

Foreword

Dr. Arthur Laffer

Today's economy reminds me so much of the late 1970s: high inflation, high interest rates, high energy prices, low levels of employment sandwiched between a recent recession, and a looming recession, and a lack of confidence in a strikingly inept president.

In 1980, Jimmy Carter lost his bid for reelection (for obvious reasons). The American electorate is not kind to presidents who preside over poor and declining economic conditions. Ronald Reagan convincingly won 44 out of 50 states, ushering in a new era for America based on competence, hope, optimism, and confidence, which materialized into one of the strongest economies in US history. Mr. Reagan implemented an appealing and workable set of policies known as supply-side economics, which reduced income tax rates and simplified the tax code, reduced the strangling regulations of government, turned rampant inflation, and boosted free trade. What more could be asked?

I am proud to say that as a close advisor to Mr. Reagan, I was honored to play a role in both the conceptualization and the implementation of supply-side economics (also known as Reaganomics). I am also proud to say that it really worked. Government revenue doubled during our eight years in office. Inflation dramatically declined, and employment soared. Supply-side economics ushered in a long expansion during the 1980s which, after a brief interruption in 1990-1991, continued full force until the recession of 2001. The foundation was laid for what was, at the time, the longest expansion in American history.

Most important, supply-side economics solved stagflation (i.e., the simultaneous occurrence of high unemployment and high inflation.) For us economists, this was a new and quite worrisome phenomenon. Economic theory as taught in universities implied that the economy can be buffeted by high unemployment, for which we have a set of ready-made policies, or inflation, for which we also have a set of ready-made policies, but not both simultaneously. Academics had no answer for stagflation.

Supply-side economics solved stagflation on both fronts, and in so doing we learned that stagflation just doesn't happen but is the result of misguided economic policies. Stagflation was so painful for ordinary Americans experiencing excessive joblessness and higher prices; and its reasons so clearly understood that I naturally assumed that no government would ever allow stagflation to reappear. I thought that stagflation would be relegated forever to the history books and to the back pages of economics texts for future students to learn how economic mismanagement can disrupt the lives of ordinary Americans.

But here we go again. High inflation, rising interest rates, high energy prices, reduced living standards for the middle class, a looming recession, and a seemingly inept president who really does not understand the deeper issues and the underlying causes of today's problems. Our current president does not have the acumen to implement the right policies to solve our myriad of problems. He also cannot seem to empathize with ordinary Americans who are constantly fretting over high prices everywhere.

Perhaps because I am an outsider looking in, I can clearly see the parallels with the economic mess of the late 1970s. I can clearly see that today's problems are self-inflicted: a bloated government that never seems to stop spending other people's money, an explosive growth in the money supply by our central bank and its callous willingness to inflict high interest rates on the American people who are already suffering from high inflation. And, as an outsider looking in, I can clearly see that the only way out of this mess is policies well-grounded in supply-side economics.

In the 1980s we were the Party with ideas. Our ideas worked and they resonated with the American people. Supply-side economics solved our problems and put Americans back to work. Our respect for the American people was reciprocated by their love for us.

Unfortunately, the ideals of sound economic policy amongst our leaders in Washington eventually dissolved and our supply-side accomplishments began to fade. As was the case in the final moments of the Carter administration, now is the time for a resurgence of pro-growth, supply-side economic policy.

With this in mind, I was very pleased to read Mr. Johnson's book. Not only do his ideas evidence a good understanding of the causes of our current problems, but his solutions are soundly based on workable economic theory. Perry seems to be one of the few Republicans who took our defeat very seriously in 2020, recognizing that in order to regain the White House in 2024, we must be the party of workable ideas that resonate with all Americans.

A key tenet of supply-side economics is that incentives matter. This is what motivates us to work harder and to save more and invest, and to provide a better life for ourselves and for our families. But, as Perry documents in *Two Cents*, our government has actually disincentivized us from working and from saving and investing. It is time to stop this. We need, as Ronald Reagan said, to get the government off our backs and we need to reinstate positive incentives for all people.

Doing so is what *Two Cents* is all about. Mr. Johnson understands the key role of incentives. He understands that the right incentives will motivate Americans to work. That the right incentives will reduce supply-side bottlenecks, enabling our businesses to produce more, thereby alleviating long-run inflation. He understands that too much money without enough goods will always lead to inflation. Mr. Johnson understands that it is imperative to reduce the size of the government, and has offered an effective policy to do so, which by the way, is a personal favorite of mine: reduce the size of discretionary government spending by 2 percent every year by incentivizing the managers of such departments with a cash bonus. How can this not work?

Americans are looking for policies that directly address their situation. Americans are looking for polices that work. Americans are looking for someone who speaks their language and understands their pain. Mr. Johnson's *Two Cents* delivers. His policies will lay the foundation for a long continuous economic expansion, just like we did during the 1980s.

Acknowledgments

My three wonderful children inspired me to write this book. I believe our country is moving in the wrong direction and that we can correct some of the miscalculations that have proved costly. There have been many people that have contributed to this book, but I owe particular thanks to Dr. Arthur Laffer, the eminent economist, for his insight. I would also like to thank my loving wife for her untiring support in all my endeavors.

Preface

I have been lucky to experience many of life's joys. I have three wonderful children who are the joy of my life and am married to the most wonderful woman on the planet. These are not empty words. My wife is my confidant, and my best friend. Every day when I come home from work my heart beams when she greets me. I am so thankful to have been blessed with a wonderful partner with whom I can share my life. Raising these three children together has made this bond even stronger.

I grew up in a middle-class family. My dad was a pilot in WWII, and my mom was a nurse in the Army WACS. They met in Europe at a New Year's Eve party which was the luckiest day of my life, otherwise I would not be here today. They loved this country and taught me that in America anything is possible. They told me, "You determine your future. Being successful in America requires nothing more than optimism and hard work." I believed them and I try to instill that principle in my children. But obviously one key to allowing people to lead great lives and achieve their dreams is a successful economy, and this is where we are now falling short.

A successful economy is fundamental to the success of any country. Without a vibrant economy its citizens cannot live the kind of life that they would like. After all, everyone needs the basic necessities of life. No matter where you go, people always love their families and their children and want to provide a better world for them. A vibrant economy is essential to providing a better world.

In the past America has done an extraordinary job of fulfilling many of the needs of its citizens. However, recent costly mistakes and miscalculations on the part of the government have had a severe negative impact on most people, particularly the middle class. Excessive inflation has negatively impacted everyone. I went to the grocery store the other day and thought I was in another country. I could not believe the cost of a head of lettuce or a pound of cherries. What I found particularly amazing is not only the increased the prices, but also the reduced the size of the package and amount you receive. Pretty soon we will have to buy potatoes individually because the bag will be too expensive!

This was caused by the government's decision to cut back on oil production. This made the cost of transporting our food from the producer to the grocery store to increase exponentially. As a result, the store has no choice but to increase their prices. The government has gone out of their way to make things as expensive as possible by reducing the supply of oil and by throwing a whole lot of money into the economy. It has hurt everyone, but particularly the middle class. Keep in mind the middle class does not receive any government assistance. They do not qualify for food stamps or housing supplements, so they must pay for these increases themselves. And this on top of the extraordinary increase in the cost of college education. In short, the middle class is getting strangled economically.

This inflation has forced the Federal Reserve to raise interest rates to levels unseen in over twenty years. This makes housing virtually unaffordable to many. This calamity was self-induced by government actions. We can correct this problem by using a more rational approach in running our government. Government departments have all been encouraged to spend every penny they have, so that they can get more added to their budget in the following year. The bigger the budget the more powerful the agency. An effort should be made to shrink our government instead of expanding it. Instead, I suggest we give the money back to the people who have earned it. In this book I discuss exactly how to do just that and get everyone back to enjoying life the way they should.

CHAPTER 1

Introduction

There has never been another country like ours, a melting pot of cultures and nationalities. Collectively we have worked together to build the greatest economy the world has ever known. Our most valuable asset in this great nation of ours is not the land, buildings, or minerals, but rather our people. Without each and every one of us, without our skills, talents, and ingenuity, there would be no resources, no means of creating wealth, and no economy.

**MY TWO-CENTS PLAN
ON IGNITING THE ECONOMY**

Reduce inflation, eliminate illegal immigration, and shrink the government to return the money to the taxpayer.

Creating wealth for all to benefit is a hallmark of our great nation; it is what we have always done. It is what sets America apart. Attracting, fostering, and incentivizing our entrepreneurial spirit is what America is all about, and has made America what it is today. We must never forget this. We must never again let the federal government debase our will to succeed and dis-incentivize us from doing what we have always done: from doing what we do best.

A key component for success is (and always will be) motivation. We are motivated to succeed. We are a country built on motivation. When my son, Perry Jr., was a three-year-old preschooler, he refused the work assigned by the teacher, which he thought was silly. Then his teacher decided to incentivize him. Every day when he would complete his work, he would get a sticker in his book. From that moment on, you could not drive him out of the class until he had successfully finished his work.

Just like Perry Jr., aren't we all motivated to succeed when we get something in return? It can be money, recognition, status, praise, or even a sticker. When we are incentivized, we become more motivated. This motivation drives us to succeed.

This is the American way. Our eternal optimism—incentivized with benefits, monetary or otherwise—has produced our great economic miracle.

The absence of incentives, or in some cases the existence of disincentives, is a great demotivator. It can engender and perpetuate stagnation. This is something that occurs in every endeavor of life from sports to the classroom to the living room to the boardroom. I have always believed that motivation is a key component to both a thriving organization and to a great country.

Here is just one example of what is happening to our country today.

We have saddled our oil and gas companies with burdensome and unnecessary regulations and restrictions. It is important to realize that America is number one in the world in keeping our environment green when refining and extracting oil and natural gas (see Chapter Four). No nation does a better job of controlling methane emissions than the USA. Whenever anyone buys oil elsewhere, they are doing the world a disservice.

Keep in mind that we have not stopped driving and we have not stopped flying. By increasing regulations on our oil and gas industries, we—along with everyone else—are forced to buy oil from other nations. We all live on the same earth. If Russia is contaminating and polluting our earth with methane emissions, the impact is felt by the entire world, including Americans. This is disastrous for our planet.

President Biden's approach, from his first day in office, has actually prevented us from producing more oil and natural gas and simultaneously hurt the environment!

Any transition to a future energy regime takes time. A lot of time! Richard Rhodes in his insightful book, *Energy: A Human History*, tells us that in past energy transitions, (i.e., from water to wood to coal to oil) it took 40 to 50 years for an energy source to go from a 1 percent market share to a 10 percent market share, and another century for the source to reach 50 percent. In the meantime, the *existing sources of energy continue to be used*! As I discuss in Chapter 4, we are a long way from achieving this goal with renewable sources of energy. Unless we want to completely stop all activities that use oil and natural gas, unless we want to stop driving and flying, and unless we want to completely drive our economy to a halt, we must continue to use our current sources of energy. We must do this in a sensible way.

The government's goal should be to incentivize us to succeed. The current administration's policies have done just the opposite.

Let's reward people and businesses for achieving. I believe that one of the ways of doing so is rewarding people for their hard work.

In this book I will lay out a plan that I think will get America back on track. The Biden administration's approach since his first day in office has been crushing to the middle class. The average family is spending 46 percent or more of their paycheck on the necessities of life: transportation, food, and shelter (see chapters 2 and 10). This leaves much less for discretionary spending. We must keep in mind when the government strangles our oil and natural gas companies with unnecessary and burdensome regulations, it raises the price of oil, and it forces us to pay more for gas and food because of higher transportation costs. When the government (and the Federal Reserve) throws a lot of money into the economy, as has occurred under Biden, it causes inflation. High inflation is one of the most disastrous things that can happen to an economy. To prevent this, the Federal Reserve has stepped in and raised interest rates. They have to persevere until inflation ceases. This is devastating to everyone but particularly the middle class.

Our current predicament was entirely caused by the government and the Federal Reserve. They spent too much money and injected more money into the economy than we had the ability to support through the output of goods and services. We are paying for this now—all of us! The government loves to spend your money. In fact, the overall prestige of a governmental department is often determined by the size of its budget. When they are allocated more money, they are deemed to be more important. In government everyone goes out of their way to spend their budget every year. This is one of the only ways they can get an increase in their budget the following year.

You are better at spending your money than the government. I am proposing that we save this country by making a radical change. I propose that we give less money to the government and more money to the people. I am suggesting that we incentivize the government to spend less, and in that process, let Americans keep more of the money that they earn.

I offer a uniquely viable (and much-needed) economic plan that will reverse this malaise, and rescue America and Americans by:

- Restoring accountability and quality to the federal government.

- Letting the people who earn the money keep more of it.

- Reducing the budget of every discretionary program by two percent annually and returning the savings directly to the people.

- Incentivizing government managers to reduce their budget. This is the best way (and perhaps the only way) to incentivize the federal government to increase the quality of the programs it delivers.

- Enabling us to become energy independent.

- Restoring faith in our oil and gas companies to become world leaders in reducing greenhouse gas emissions. Recognizing that our economy must be based on a sensible energy plan, rooted in our current energy availability. Recognizing this is a necessary ingredient to reduce long-run inflation.

- Incentivizing and motivating Americans to do what we do best: innovate.

- Effectively downsizing an ever-growing government that saps our strength and return the resources to the American people. Reducing long-run inflation.

- Reducing and simplifying the tax code.

Founded over 250 years ago, the United States of America has become a shining beacon among nations, a successful experiment in the annals of humanity. But like the unfinished pyramid on the back of our dollar bill, we have yet to reach our potential, thanks to an ever-intrusive government. No wonder many of us are frustrated and are filled with angst.

Why should we be content with an ever-growing government that saps our strength? Our federal government is incentivized to spend as much as possible each year, for the larger the budget the more powerful the agency. Instead of being incentivized to spend less, they are incentivized to spend more—more of *your* money, which you rightfully have earned.

Why should we burden our energy companies with unnecessary regulations and supply-side restrictions when they are currently global leaders in reducing greenhouse gas emissions? We are the world leader in protecting the environment when it comes to drilling and refining oil, but the Biden administration has done everything in its power (and more) to stifle the USA's energy production, and as a result, the Biden administration has *increased* the world's fossil fuel emissions.

Where is the logic in shutting down the Keystone pipeline, and incentivizing less oil and gas drilling, when regardless of our long-term goals, we need to continue to rely on fossil fuels now?

Why should we allow and put up with porous national borders, encouraging a record-breaking number of illegal immigrants, which creates discontent and weakens our national security? As well as makes a mockery of our concern with law and order?

Instead, the Biden administration restricts *legal* immigration. We might be the only country that favors illegal over legal immigration. Why are we incentivizing *illegal* immigration when we should be encouraging *legal* immigration? Why make it so difficult for legal immigrants to enter the USA, when they have so much to offer and have long helped build our great nation?

My Two-Cents plan proposes to reduce discretionary spending by 2 percent annually and return the money directly to the American people. I believe that we are better off letting the people who earn the money decide how to spend it. This the essence of a democracy. This is what capitalism is all about.

I want to introduce laissez-faire principles into the running of our government. Instead of rewarding our government managers for spending money, let's reward them for running quality and efficient operations. I propose we give a bonus to the manager(s) who cut their discretionary spending by 2 percent annually. This is one way to disincentivize our government from spending every dollar in their budget by year's end.

My Two-Cents plan will ignite our economy and improve the quality of life for all. In the late 1980s, as a result of the Jimmy Carter years, we had a similar set of problems. We had high inflation and high energy prices. This necessitated the Federal Reserve to raise interest rates to astronomical levels, in effect, causing the prime rate to reach a record 21.5 percent in December 1980.

Reaganomics solved the problem by putting the money back into hands of the people who earned the money, igniting our lackluster economy. That philosophy worked once, and it can work again.

By restoring hope and incentivizing work we will achieve our rightful place in the annals of nations while incentivizing a more democratic government that restores wealth and economic decision making to the American people.

Cartoon 1 – Fly on the Wall

My Two-Cents plan is a practical, easily understood book that can (and should) be read by *every* citizen. It will help all Americans to understand the issues confronting us at this critical point in our history. It will help all of us make America better.

Each of the book's twelve chapters discusses some important problems Americans currently face. These include inflation, jobs, energy, illegal immigration, Social Security and Medicare, federal deficit and increasing debt, discretionary spending, productivity, and increasing tax burden. This book illustrates some of the flaws of the Biden administration. Naturally, I cannot address all the issues, and I am sure there will be more by the time this book is published. In addition to discussing the problems, I offer practical Two-Cents plan solutions that can effectively make America better.

In the early 1980s we had just come off the disastrous Carter administration with record high inflation, high energy costs, and rising interest rates. The automobile industry was getting crushed because Japan was beating us in quality, while taking away sizable market share.

Back then, I knew how to solve the quality problem, and I did. I introduced techniques that eventually became the standard around the world. I literally wrote the book on quality—*ISO 9000,* published by McGraw Hill—which continues to be widely read and is now in its third edition. My companies, Perry Johnson Registrars and Perry Johnson Laboratory Accreditation, do business in sixty-one countries around the world.

I intend to use my successful experience in industry to help solve the problems caused by the federal government's economic mismanagement.

It is important to note that I am not an overspender. I own more than seventy companies, none of which have any debt! I do not have any personal debt. If any of my companies need any funding, it comes directly from me personally.

Although I had a happy childhood, my parents did not have money to send me to college. I started with nothing and remember getting eviction notices regularly while in graduate school. I knew what it was like to have my gas and electricity shut off and not have enough food to eat. I come from the school of hard knocks and can very much relate to the travails of average Americans.

When I started my first company nobody gave or lent me any money. Like most entrepreneurs, I struggled unmercifully the first couple of years, putting in eighty-hour work weeks without making a dime, but I knew in my heart that I would succeed. Like your typical entrepreneur, I had (and still have!) unbridled optimism—the fire that drove me then and still drives me today. That fire is called the American spirit. The Biden administration has done everything in its power (and more) to squelch it. My Two-Cents plan is all about reviving that American fire and proposes how to do it. We want to incentivize and motivate Americans to succeed. In this way we will get our country back on track.

We need short-term action and long-term smarts. *Two Cents to Save America* delivers both.

CHAPTER 2

Taming Inflation

B
y December 1848, one percent of the American population had migrated to California—the largest migration in US history— searching for gold and instant wealth. By 1855, about 750,000 pounds of gold, worth over $12 billion today, was extracted, with most of it circulating in the area and adding to the local economy. Guess what happened to prices?

**MY TWO-CENTS PLAN
ON INFLATION**

Discourage, disincentivize, and end policies that contribute to inflation, while emphasizing supply-side policies that will ensure adequate production of goods with inexpensive energy.

One reporter at the time tells of breakfasting with a friend on bread, cheese, butter, sardines, and two bottles of beer. He was shocked to receive a bill for $43 ($1,200 in today's prices). Canteens sold slices of buttered bread for $56 apiece in today's prices; a dozen eggs cost the equivalent of $90; a pound of coffee cost $1,200; and a pair of decent working boots was $3,000.[1]

Gamblers coming into the area were charged $10,000 (in today's prices) a night for a room. And this was not the Beverly Hills Hotel.

The rooms had no bathrooms and were only 160 square feet. There is the story of a woman making over $18,000 selling pies to the miners and of an individual selling hundreds of newspapers from back east to the miners for one dollar each. (Newspaper in those days typically cost no more than two cents.) The owner of several hardware stores who had profited enormously by hoarding all the necessary miner's tools (buckets, pans, shovels) sold them to desperate miners for wildly inflated prices.[2]

Cartoon 2 – Cost of Breakfast

Needless to say, the miners were shocked, amazed, and bewildered by such high (and unexpected) prices. So are Americans today. Can we really say that we are better off when the prices of most goods have substantially increased? Let's face it. Our incomes have not kept pace with rising prices. What makes it particularly bad for us is that higher interest rates are causing our housing costs to soar.

By October 2022 America was saddled with an 8 percent annual rate of inflation, the highest since 1981 (see Figure 2.1). Grocery prices have risen 12 percent annually, the fastest pace since 1979; gasoline prices have risen 60 percent over the past year. Rents have increased by 5.8 percent annually, the highest increase since 1986. Inflation has affected everyone, especially the middle class, who tend to spend a greater share of their income on food and energy.

Figure 2.1 US *Inflation Rate, 1950-2022*

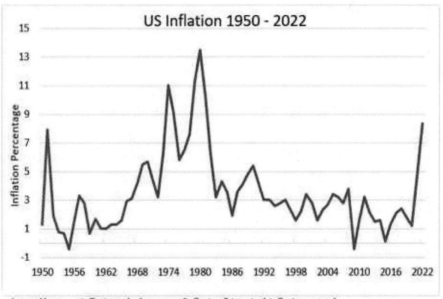

https://www.usinflationcalculator.com/inflation/historical-inflation-rates/

Inflation eats away at our ability to spend. It dampens our psyche and whittles away our optimism and confidence in the future. It also shrinks the value of stocks, particularly for firms with a relatively large debt. Inflation is our number one problem, and it should be the number one concern for policymakers.

The reason should be painfully obvious to all Americans: rising prices reduce our standard of living. We all feel its pinch and the pain. When I worked in Brazil, inflation was so ridiculously rampant that store owners were constantly raising prices. One time after picking out something for purchase and while walking to the register, the store owner increased the price! Such runaway inflation, although certainly not unique to Brazil (Weimar Germany, Turkey, and Argentina come to mind), forces people to spend their money as soon as it is earned, otherwise it becomes worth less and in the extreme even *worthless*.

To avoid that situation here in the USA, the Federal Reserve, our central bank, has no choice but to slow the economy down by raising interest rates, which, as I discuss below, causes further pain and suffering. Thanks to higher interest rates, for example, the monthly cost of a new home purchased with a mortgage has increased by 40 percent since Biden took office.

For an economy to work we need inflation at a low level. The ideal mark should be 2 percent. When the rate of inflation gets above that level the economy does not work as it should. N. Gregory Mankiw, the former chairperson of the President's Council of Economic Advisors under George Bush (2003-2005), and author of a popular introductory economics textbook explains:

> Money, as the economy's unit of account, is what we use to quote prices and record debts. In other words, money is the yardstick with which we measure economic transactions. The job of the Federal Reserve is a bit like the job of the Bureau of Standards—to ensure the reliability of a commonly used unit of measurement. When the Fed increases the money supply and creates inflation, it erodes the real value of the unit of account.[3]

Inflation is a disorienting fog that makes one lose his or her bearings. Inflation distorts the useful information contained in relative prices.[4] With inflation, and especially when it is high, no one knows why prices are increasing, how long the price increases will continue, nor the real value of goods and services. The longer that inflation continues, the more damage done to our economy:

> The tax code incorrectly measures real incomes in the presence of inflation... accountants incorrectly measure firms' earnings when prices are rising over time. Because inflation causes dollars at different times to have different real values, computing a firm's profit... is more complicated in an economy with inflation... inflation makes investors less able to sort successful firms from unsuccessful firms, impeding financial markets in their role of allocating the economy's saving among alternative types of investment.[5]

And of course, let's not forget that ordinary consumers always suffer the most under inflation.

What Happened in Argentina?

In the extreme, inflation grinds an economy to a halt. Take a look at Argentina, where inflation is already at 64 percent and is expected to reach 90 percent by December 2022.[6] Argentina has struggled with inflation over the last fifty years. Martin Feldstein, President Reagan's chief economic adviser, and chairperson of his Council of Economic Advisors from 1982 to 1984, tells us that in Argentina "from 1975 to 1990, the annual [inflation] rate averaged a remarkable 300 percent, meaning that the price level doubled every few months, on average. Prices rose at an explosive annual rate of more than 1,000 percent in 1989."[7]

How do individuals survive under such circumstances? How does the nation survive? Since 2018, the Argentinian inflation rate has topped 30 percent every year. What is it like for the average Argentinian?

- Consumers spend their pesos as quickly as they get them, which by the way, abets existing shortages. Buying fast and quickly is how to stay one step ahead of inflation.

- Consumers avoid banks and do not use credit cards, and they buy in installments. The act of saving, so crucial in any economy, ceases to exist.

- Menus are constantly changing; taxi meters are frequently adjusted; and price tags are almost immediately outdated.

- Producers hold off supplying goods, anticipating that prices will only rise in the future. Why supply now, when one can do so later and more profitably?

- Everyone who can afford to, uses the black market to obtain US dollars, with most sellers (especially in real estate) only accepting dollars.

- Argentinians without access to dollars live in poverty or close to it (the poverty rate is now 37 percent, up from 30 percent in 2016) trapped in jobs whose wages are not automatically linked to higher prices. They are forced to collect scraps to sell and participate in collectives where goods and services are swapped, obviating the need to use the peso.

So how did this happen? Part of Argentina's recent inflation uptick is due to the same forces that have been affecting the world over: rising energy prices, the war in Ukraine, and supply-side constraints. But the deeper, underlying causes of Argentina's inflation are self-inflicted. The nation spends far more than it receives in revenue. The government funds everything from health care to university education, to public transportation. It makes up the shortfall between spending and revenue by printing money. The more pesos printed relative to the goods and services available, the greater the increase in prices.

Once prices begin to rise, people expect them to continue, so businesses post higher prices and workers demand higher wages—everyone wants to get on the bandwagon, so to speak. Anticipating higher prices, consumers buy now rather than later, and businesses postpone selling their products in anticipation of higher future prices. All of which exacerbates existing shortages and further increases inflation, causing workers to demand higher compensation and businesses to raise prices, continuing the upward spiral. By the way, severe inflation never ends kindly. Some type of drastic action is usually taken: the currency is devalued, interest rates are driven sky high, or in the worst cases (think of Weimar Germany) a political revolution occurs.

We do not want what happened in Argentina to happen in America. We can stop inflation but only at great cost. But before we discuss this, it is important to recognize that we have done this to ourselves. Our inflation is self-induced.

We Did This Inflation to Ourselves

Yes, that is right: we did this to ourselves. Well, not exactly *we*. The government did this. You and I had nothing to do with it. But ordinary Americans are suffering its punishing effects. Worse yet, ordinary Americans are suffering the effects of the Fed's preferred "solution" to inflation: higher interest rates (more on this later in the chapter).

But how could this have happened? Didn't we learn the lessons from the California Gold Rush? Why did our government ignore one of humankind's most studied lessons: too much money chasing too few goods increases prices?

Indeed, so many examples abound of the destructive effects of inflation that it is inexcusable to claim ignorance. In ancient Rome, soldiers often complained about higher prices wherever they marched, resulting in the Roman emperor Diocletian in AD 302 issuing his famous edict, "Let there be cheapness." In sixteenth century Spain explorers brought home tons of gold and silver (literally). Three guesses as to what happened to prices? In Weimar, Germany, an incompetent government relentlessly pumped money into the economy to pay for programs and to appease an increasingly restless public. We all know how that story ended.

If these unambiguously clear-cut lessons were not enough, the after-effects of every virus, pandemic, and epidemic in the annals of human history have been assiduously studied, and guess what was found? In addition to the human tragedy and suffering, supply bottlenecks occurred, pent-up demand was released, and with widespread shortages of goods and services, wages and prices increased (sometimes sharply) resulting in inflation.[8] No exceptions!

Today's COVID-19 is certainly no different: consumers unleashed a wave of pent-up spending. Inflation increased in the face of supply cutbacks and supply chain bottlenecks, spurred by enormous, unprecedented federal spending and ultra-low borrowing costs. No surprise.

In August 2022, at the annual gathering of the world's central bankers in Jackson Hole, Wyoming, Jerome Powell, chair of the USA Federal Reserve (our central bank) said that "without price stability, the economy does not work for anyone."[9]

Agreed. But Mr. Powell should have added that the government and the Federal Reserve[10] caused this bout of recent inflation, through excessive fiscal spending, and careful economic mismanagement. So how did we get ourselves into the mess? Four reasons:

Reason #1: An unprecedented sharp growth in the money supply.

Figure 2.2 illustrates the increase in the money supply,[11] defined by M1 and M2, where M stands for money, and 1 indicates the highest liquidity (i.e., it is readily usable by consumers). M2 is slightly less liquid than M1.

Figure 2.2 The USA increase in the money supply, measured by M1 and M2.

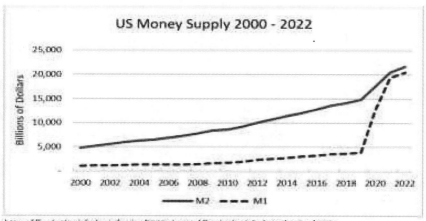

https://fred.stlouisfed.org/series/M2SL https://fred.stlouisfed.org/series/GDP

The money supply has increased by 40 percent during the Biden administration, representing the largest increase in money supply in US history. According to the Fed, the recent splurge in the money supply (actually beginning in 2019) was necessary to immediately rescue the American economy and to prevent another Great Depression. But alas, this was like a doctor prescribing a medication while ignoring its long-term effects, which they were surely aware of, but deciding to go ahead with the "cure" anyway.

During COVID, with interest rates almost zero (more on this soon) and the cost of borrowing ridiculously cheap, the amount of money circulating in our economy increased dramatically (see Figure 2.2). Just like during the California Gold Rush, money never sits idle; it is used to buy (or at least demand) goods and services, and if there are not enough (which was surely the case in 2020-2021, as during most, if not all, post-viruses in human history), inflation inevitably results.

Cartoon 3 – Biden the Rain Man

Reason #2: Sharp increase in federal government spending.

For more or less the same reasons that the money supply increased, so did government spending over the same period. Figure 2.3 illustrates this quite nicely.

The recent sharp increase in federal spending began during the Trump administration, followed by the Biden administration dishing out stimulus payments, extending unemployment insurance, increasing public health spending, and extending loans and grants to businesses.

At a time when it was obvious that we had already injected a lot of money into the economy to try to extricate ourselves from the COVID crisis, the Biden administration decided to open the floodgates. What happened was the biggest spending spree in history surpassing the spending of WWII. Add to this the $550-billion Infrastructure Bill (November 2021), the $349-billion Inflation Reduction Act (July 28, 2022), and the $52-billion CHIPS for America Act (July 28, 2022), and you have a whopping increase in federal spending. Who knows what other massive bills will be passed in the remaining years of the Biden administration? It is estimated that about half of the recent inflation increase is due to excessive fiscal spending, or effective economic mismanagement.[12]

Figure 2.3 US federal government spending, 1949-2021

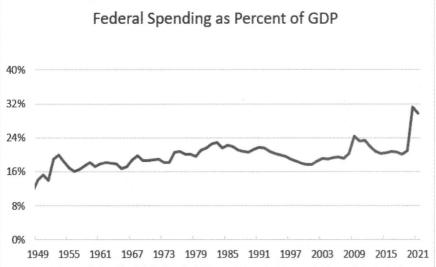

https://www.rug.nl/ggdc/historicaldevelopment/maddison/releases/maddison-project-database-2020?lang=en https://www.presidency.ucsb.edu/statistics/data/federal-budget-receipts-and-outlays https://www.whitehouse.gov/omb/budget/historical-tables/
https://www.usinflationcalculator.com/inflation/historical-inflation-rates/

As businesses locked down during COVID and laid off workers, and as consumers did not go out, the economy came to a standstill. The Fed and the federal government called for drastic action to keep the economy afloat. But that is like a doctor prescribing medication while ignoring the painful side effects. Although in this case the "doctors" were well aware of the side effects. To be more specific, inflation will result if we:

- Increase stimuli, without an attendant increase in the available goods and services.

- Increase federal spending, while ignoring supply-side restrictions and bottlenecks.

No exceptions.

Cartoon 4 – The Yolks on Us?

Reason #3: Arrogance, hubris, and a present-oriented vision.

The following illustrative quote, written in December 2020, eight months after the recession 'officially' ended[13] in April 2020, but before the recent bout of inflation kicked in, is worth quoting in full:

> Economists love to disagree, but almost all of them will tell you that inflation is dead. The premise of low inflation is baked into economic policies and financial markets. It is why central banks can cut interest rates to around zero and buy up mountains of government bonds. It explains how governments have been able to go on an epic spending and borrowing binge in order to save the economy from the ravages

of the pandemic—and why rich-world public debt of 125 percent barely raises an eyebrow.[14]

But the authors had the good sense to write:

> Yet [there is] an increasingly vocal band of dissenters that the world could emerge from the pandemic into an era of higher inflation. [So] rather than ignore the risk, governments should take action now to ensure themselves against it.

Needless to say, our government ignored the risk *and* took no action. Even worse, their policies only added fuel to the fire.

The Fed, aware of the inflation potential, underestimated its possibility, assuming that the supply-side kinks would soon work themselves out (not all central banks did). Testifying before Congress, February 23, 2020, Mr. Powell dismissed the upsurge in the money supply as "not having really important implications." Writing in July 2020, Greenwood and Hanke noted that,

> Reporting about U.S. inflation rarely contains the words 'money supply.' We are repeatedly told that the most recent upticks in inflation are anomalous and 'transitory,' despite clear evidence that since March 2020, the M2 has been growing at an average annualized rate of 23.9 percent—the fastest since World War II. The inflation upticks aren't temporary and were predictable, driven by an extraordinary explosion in the money supply.[15]

But "our" Fed assumed that if inflation did occur and thought they could snuff it out with laser-like precision while magically preventing a recession.

Cartoon 5 – Biden Printing More Money

Unfortunately, and more often than not, when the Fed increases interest rates a recession occurs (think of 2007-2009, 2001, 1991-1992, 1981-1982, and 1980, just to name a few). Irina Ivanova explains the how and why:

> When rates rise […] Any consumer item that people take on debt to buy—whether… automobiles or washing machines—gets more expensive… That means less work for the people making those cars and washing machines, and eventually, layoffs. Other parts of the economy sensitive to interest rates, such as construction, home sales and mortgage refinancing, also slow down, affecting employment in that sector.
>
> In addition, people travel less, leading hotels to reduce staffing to account for lower occupancy rates. Businesses looking to expand—say, a coffee shop chain opening a new branch—are more hesitant to do so when borrowing costs are high. And as people spend less on travel,

dining out and entertainment, those hoteliers and restaurateurs will have fewer customers to serve and eventually cut back on staff.[16]

This is nothing more than the law of supply and demand, one of the most basic principles of any economy: if something becomes more expensive, people will demand less of it. Raise the cost of borrowing and people will borrow less. But when interest rates increase, it is the firms producing these products, as well as their employees who might get laid off, that suffer through no fault of their own. Nevertheless, the Federal Reserve and most of the economics profession was and is (and probably always will be) extremely confident in its main inflation-fighting tool—raising interest rates.

I am not sure about you, but sometimes I wonder why those who conduct fiscal policy (who control government spending and the rates of taxation) are elected by the people but officials conducting monetary policy (increasing/decreasing interest rates and the money supply) are not. This means that if we don't like a specific *fiscal* policy, we can vote those responsible out of office, but if we don't like a particular *monetary* policy, such as excessive money supply increase painful interest rate increases, we have no say in the matter.[17] American voters have no say in the country's monetary policy, yet all of us suffer the painful inflation and rising interest rates. How undemocratic is that?

Perhaps if monetary officials were elected and not appointed, their cavalier attitude toward the possibility of inflation (as in 2020) would not have been so cavalier, and their gung-ho attitude toward raising interest rates (as happened in 2022, and will probably happen in 2023[18]) would not have been so gung ho. Unfortunately, this "tool" always works since increasing interest rates dampens demand for big-ticket items like housing, automobiles, and anything where consumers need to borrow money, making it harder to borrow.

If interest rates increase high enough (as they usually do) firms will lay off workers due to falling demand; wages and profits will fall; unemployment will increase; and the result is a recession. Figure 2.4 illustrates this quite nicely. The columns represent recessions (the width corresponds to the recession length). Notice that without exception, every recession is precipitated by an increase (sometimes sharp) in the federal funds rate.[19] Then after the recession, the federal funds rate is decreased, which sometimes causes problems of its own, like cheap money leading to the real estate bubble in the early 2000s.

Figure 2.4 The US Federal Funds Rate and Recessions

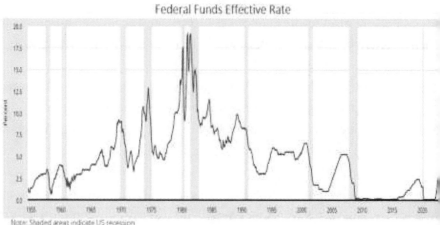

Federal Funds Effective Rate

Note: Shaded areas indicate US recession
Source: Board of Governors of the Federal Reserve System; St Louis Fed

Looking at Figure 2.4, one cannot help but wonder why the Fed does not just leave the Federal Funds Rate alone, and control interest rates and the money supply with other mechanisms. Alas, such thinking is not in the Fed's repertoire.

The Fed has so far in 2022 raised the federal funds rate three times, each by three quarters of a percent (and they are by no means done). They expect to increase rates to 4.4 percent by December 2022 and possibly 4.6 percent by early 2023—the highest level since 2007. It is a safe bet that a recession awaits (and perhaps is already underway). With a current inflation rate (as of August 2022) of 8.3 percent, the Fed has a long way to go to get the inflation rate back to its desired level of 2 percent.

So, the American taxpayer suffers a double whammy: high inflation followed by layoffs and depressed demand. We caused neither, but we insidiously suffer both.

Cartoon 6 – Biden's Money Fire Pit

As the Fed "successfully" wages its war against inflation (lauded by the press and most economists) casualties mount. Note the blunt callousness in Mr. Powell's wording: "There will very likely be some softening of labor market conditions… We will keep at it until we are confident the job is done." As Ivanova explains,

> In plain English, that means unemployment. The Fed forecasts the unemployment rate to rise to 4.4 percent next year, from 3.5 percent today—a number that implies an additional 1.2 million people losing their jobs.[20]

But do not expect the unemployment rate to conveniently come to rest at 4.4 percent, as if the Fed could magically wave a wand and stop unemployment anywhere it chooses. Bank of America, for one, expects a peak unemployment rate of 5.6 percent in 2023, putting an additional 3.2 million people out of work. Even this might be overly optimistic, especially if the Fed continues to increase interest rates into 2023. Oxford Economics sees almost no net hiring in the first six months of 2023, with combined job losses in the second and third quarters of 2023 at 1.7 million.[21] Wow!

So, we get the federal government increasing spending like there is no tomorrow, and the Federal Reserve practically adding money at will. Now to correct its mistakes, the Fed is raising interest rates causing economic pain for all. If Dante were alive today and writing his *Inferno*, he would surely include high interest rates and high unemployment as one of the rings of hell.

But wait, we're not done. After admitting that his policies will cause unemployment, Mr. Powell said, "I wish there were a painless way to do that, there isn't." Come on Mr. Powell. Go back to 2020 and even 2019, to see some of your fellow central bankers urging caution. Go back to 2020 (and earlier) and read Milton Friedman, Arthur Laffer, and many others offering workable (and alternative) solutions.

This is the price of letting inflation get away. This is the price of not listening to others. This is the price of a narrow world view. This is the price of hubris.

Speaking of hubris, in the Fed's September 21, 2022, statement to the public explaining their reason for increasing the federal funds rate, there was no mea culpa that their actions were part of the problem:

> Recent indicators point to modest growth in spending and production. Job gains have been robust in recent months, and the unemployment rate has remained low. Inflation remains elevated, reflecting supply and demand imbalances related to the pandemic, higher food and energy prices, and broader price pressures. Russia's war against

Ukraine is causing tremendous human and economic hardship. The war and related events are creating additional upward pressure on inflation and are weighing on global economic activity. The Committee [the Federal Open Market Committee[22]] is highly attentive to inflation risks [and] anticipates that ongoing increases in the target range will be appropriate. (FOMC Press Release, 2022)

Stay tuned!

One of the biggest causalities in the inflation war is the housing market. So far this year, the owners' equivalent rent, a proxy for shelter, has risen 6.2 percent, which is the highest since 1983.[23] Since 2021, mortgage rates have doubled (as of this writing), and most likely will continue increasing. This reduces new home sales and sales of existing homes, which in turn, negatively affects a host of related industries such as construction, household furniture and appliances, lumber yards, etc.

In 2020, the average price of a home sale in the USA was $374,500.[24] As of the second quarter 2022 it is $525,000. That is an increase of 40.2 percent. The monthly payment for principal and interest on the average home in 2020 was $1,961 per month. In early October 2022 with interest rates of 7.375 percent on a thirty-year mortgage for someone with a credit rating of 750 or higher, the monthly payment is $3,372, which does not include taxes or insurance.

That's a staggering increase of 70.4 percent in just eighteen months! This is an Argentinian-like increase in the cost of living.

Unfortunately, given the rising interest rates already underway, and the Fed's determination to keep raising them until inflation is tamed and the economy subdued, expect these numbers to continue to increase. On the basis of this troubling statistic alone, we can safely say that Americans are worse off today because of Bidenomics.

Cartoon 7 – The Incredible Shrinking House

But stick around, unfortunately, in terms of statistics we are just getting started.

The Economist cites four reasons why inflation might be here to stay:

- Since 2000, public debt has soared across the rich nations. This fuels the fear that central banks will at some point have to print money to finance this debt. This fear boosts inflationary expectations, which in turn increases current inflation. Once inflation expectations get cemented into our psyche, they are very difficult to dislodge.

- The COVID fiscal stimuli, implemented by governments across the world, restored confidence in governments' ability to use fiscal stimulus. This over-confidence sets the stage for our federal government to use fiscal stimuli in the future. Like the first reason, this increases inflationary expectations.

- Workers are becoming scarcer, due to aging and a slowing population growth. This affects all western nations, including the USA. This scarcity will continue to put upward pressure on wage rates.

- Unlike the 1980s and 1990s when free trade led to significant productivity improvements, today's greater nationalism, higher tariffs, greater uncertainty, fallout from COVID, and greater geopolitical uncertainty have reduced trade-induced productivity gains.[25]

As discussed in the next section, my Two-Cents plan policies recognize these causes as well as the causes of higher energy prices. Basing policies on a thorough understanding of the underlying causes is the only way to conduct economic policy—which continues to remain foreign to the Biden administration.

Let's Not Forget About the Supply Side

While the cause of demand-induced inflation (too much money chasing too few goods) is relatively easy to grasp, that of supply-side inflation is less so, but just as important. More specifically, if it costs more to supply the same amount of goods and services, then all else equal, inflation will increase. Today, COVID-induced absences have hampered production and increased shipping time; supply chains have broken down, causing innumerable delays; and increases in the cost of energy have exacerbated the upward inflationary cycle.

Central to my Two-Cents plan is reducing the cost of energy production, an important topic which merits its own chapter (see chapter 4). Here, I would just like to mention that increasing energy costs, which have so frustrated American consumers, have underlying causes—they did not just happen. The Biden administration's burdensome regulations and unnecessary supply-side restrictions have significantly increased the cost of producing oil and natural gas. This was

thoughtlessly done to somehow magically carry us to the golden age of
renewable energy while conveniently forgetting that the USA, and the
world for that matter, still heavily relies on fossil fuels.

We have high energy prices because of a shortage of supply relative
to demand. When demand is greater than supply, price increases. Nothing more than economics 101. You only have one person to thank.
Three guesses!

Cartoon 8 – Perry Johnson at a Grocery Store

Inflation Is Everywhere

One of our most famous economists and Nobel laureate, Milton
Freidman,[26] fancied displaying one of the oldest relationships in economics on his license plate: MV = PY. It is an identity, meaning it is
always and everywhere true by definition. On the left we have M,
which equals the money supply (either M1 or M2), and V, the velocity
of money, or how many transactions a dollar bill makes (i.e., "the

turnover rate of a dollar through the US economy."[27]) On the right, we have the nation's price level (P) multiplied by Y, its real GDP (i.e., how much stuff the economy is actually producing).

We obtain a good insight into the usefulness of this equation (and why Milton Friedman stuck it on his license plate) if we either assume Y is at full capacity, meaning all our economy's resources are fully utilized and the economy cannot produce anymore, or as happened during COVID, the supply of goods and services remains fixed, or even declines. If we assume that velocity is constant, which is quite reasonable, then increases in the money supply will directly lead to increases in the price level.[28]

Greenwood and Hanke summarize nicely how this equation works today:

> Plug today's numbers into the model and solve for M, and money supply (M2) should be growing at around 6 percent a year for the Fed to hit its inflation target of 2 percent. With M2 growing at nearly four times the "ideal" rate since March 2020, inflation is baked into the cake, and it's likely to persist. By the end of the year, the year-over-year inflation rate will be at least 6 percent and possibly as high as 9 percent. While velocity did collapse with the onset of Covid, it's on track to pick up until the end of 2024. Consequently, velocity will grease the monetary wheels. That's why inflation might hit the high end of our forecast range.[29]

Greenwood and Hanke conclude, "Mr. Powell and his colleagues should start paying attention to the money supply. Money matters. Indeed, it dominates." Agreed! The historical evidence substantiates this claim. Both the Federal Reserve and Joe Biden have done everything in their power (and more) to increase federal spending and the money supply without first increasing the amount of goods and services produced.

I feel that the best solution for inflation is not to let it happen in the first place. After all, we have countless examples over hundreds of years to fully understand its causes. The secret of good government is not to let the inflation horse leave the barn in the first place. But once done (as is the case now), perhaps the only solution is for the Fed to raise interest rates, as they are doing now. Although this works, it comes at a tremendously high cost. But not to do anything in the face of rising prices invites hyperinflation—an even worse situation fueled by expectations that inflation will continue, and nothing will be done to stop it.

Policies to Reduce Inflation

Inflation reduces our ability to spend, it dampens our psyche, it whittles away our optimism and confidence in the future, and, as Friedrich Hayek and so many others have noted, inflation chips away at the very foundation of our capitalist economy. My Two-Cents plan polices will reign in the runaway inflation horse. Although I just list them here, they will be fully developed in the upcoming chapters:

- By incentivizing the will to work, my Two-Cents plan will increase the labor force participation rate, thereby increasing federal revenue while, at the same time, reducing means-tested spending such as Medicaid and welfare spending (See chapter 3).

- Increase our labor force, which will in turn, alleviate pressure on wages and prices, and labor supply bottlenecks (see chapters 3 and 6).

- Reduce unnecessary and burdensome regulations and supply-side restrictions on USA oil and natural gas producers. This will increase our supply of energy, thereby easing inflationary pressures, while reducing our global warming gases (see chapter 4).

- Reduce discretionary spending 2 percent across the board and return the money directly to the people (see chapters 3 and 8). This will prompt greater labor force participation, more innovative and entrepreneurial activity, and economic growth. As the labor force increases, the economy grows; and as the economy grows, so does the labor force.

- Increase the productivity of supply side factors (see chapters 4 and 9).

Before we discuss these policies in depth, we must first critique the woefully misnamed (and inept) Inflation Reduction Act.

Critique of the Inflation Reduction Act

In August 2022, the Biden administration passed the Inflation Reduction Act (IRA). Biden himself lauded it as "a godsend for American families," and Joe Manchin (Democratic Senator, West Virginia) called it "a good bill that would benefit the country."

Does this mean that we finally have a federal policy that will tackle inflation head-on and reduce inflation to the Fed's goal of a 2 percent annual rate?

The answer is a resounding no.

Despite its claim, and despite its disingenuous name, the IRA "will do next to nothing to reduce inflation, especially in the short term. The name of the bill is a transparent attempt to sell it to a public worried about soaring prices."[30]

Given its disingenuous and false claim, it is important for Americans to know exactly what the IRA attempts to do and what it does not and cannot do. This, in turn, will enable us to see clearly how my policies will help all Americans by actually reducing inflation.

When one steps away from the liberal soundbites and actually investigates the IRA's specifics, one finds nothing more than a hodgepodge of hastily constructed policies lacking an overall cohesive theme. This is a classic case of (liberal) government spending gone wrong. Rather than call it the Inflation Reduction Act, perhaps it should have been named the Misinforming Americans Act (MAA) or even better, the Inflation Increasing Act (IIA). It does nothing to actually reduce inflation!

What the IRA Does

Despite the IRA's overall messiness, we can discern four themes:

1) Raise revenue

To raise revenue the IRA proposes a 15 percent minimum tax on book income (i.e., the amount of income companies report on their financial statements to shareholders) for corporations with profits over $1 billion, beginning December 31, 2022. This would supposedly affect only 150 corporations. As the IRA's biggest revenue raiser, this tax is expected to bring in $220 billion over ten years. But economists who have long studied the issue argue that raising revenue by increasing taxes on corporations is most ineffective:

> While there is always a populist appeal to raising corporate taxes, based on the misunderstanding that the burden is somehow only felt by a small number of people, it is the job of the economists to remind people of the facts and resist political efforts that have no basis in economic reality. Corporate taxes do not come freely, but rather at the expense of more investment, more job opportunities, and higher wages. Raising corporate taxes now, at a time of economic uncertainty would be particularly irresponsible... it will distort investment and may prove to be ineffective in raising revenue."[31]

The IRA further assumes that no behavioral responses will occur, despite well-documented studies that tax increases (and price increases in general) will generate avoidance behavior. For example, if the price of a movie ticket doubles, I will most likely watch fewer movies while using Netflix more and things like that. To make matters worse, the corporate tax is levied on the corporation's book income rather than its revenue, which as *The Economist* notes "makes a messy American tax system even messier."[32] Needless to say, the actual amount collected from the IRA will be far lower, and at the very least, highly uncertain.

The Wall Street Journal reported a study conducted by researchers at the University of North Carolina Tax Center to see how much revenue would have actually been collected if the IRA were in place in 2021. The results were startling: fewer than eighty publicly traded companies would have paid any tax. The total collected would have been $32 billion, with just six companies—Amazon, Berkshire, Ford, AT&T, eBay, and Moderna—paying half of the amount.

But don't assume that that amount will be the same every year. Once the law is in place, companies will avoid paying the tax and most likely will "change behavior to minimize taxes." While Joe Biden lauded the new tax, claiming that "the days of profitable companies paying no tax are over," Jeff Hoopes, one of the study's authors noted that "who actually pays a lot is just not very many firms at all . . . we have the anti-loophole tax bill that is full of loopholes."[33]

The IRA calls for increasing IRS resources by $80 billion over ten years, which, in turn, is expected to generate $204 billion in revenue. The added resources will enable the agency to hire 87,000 new agents and double its budget by 2031 with the goal of enforcing more tax collection. As the *Orange County Register* editorializes,

> Bringing in new employees [today, about half of the current 78,000 IRS agents are eligible for retirement] and training them on the wildly complex tax code which makes the IRS not just tax collectors but a benefit agency, issuing refundable tax credits such as the Earned Income Tax Credit and the Child Tax Credit, and now a new climate credit for energy investments…The bottom line: Don't expect $204 billion in new revenue to come rolling in.[34]

Problem: Since the very rich can afford their own CPAs, it seems like the IRS will be going after the middle class, who do their best to pay their fair share of taxes. Perhaps this is the Biden administration's way of lending a helping hand to America's accountants?

Cartoon 9 – IRS Visit Biden Style

The IRA will also impose a 1 percent excise tax on the value of stock repurchases.[35] Companies repurchase stock to reward shareholders and boost shareholder price by artificially restricting supply. But this is a misguided and overly optimistic attempt to punish firms for rewarding their shareholders while naively assuming that it would raise the intended revenue, while not negatively impacting the economy. But is this really the time to tax anything which will adversely affect the stock market when markets across the world have lost approximately 20 percent of their value? Just look at your 401K.

2) Incentivize electric vehicles

The IRA would provide incentives in the form of tax credits for American consumers and American businesses to purchase more EVs. We already have a tax abatement for electric cars, with Ford, General Motors, and Tesla producing. The reality, however, is that if everyone bought an electric car right now, we would not have the supporting infrastructure. Instead, we would have a calamity on our hands. Biden feels that by crippling the oil industry it would force everyone to buy electric cars. Another example of Biden mismanagement while overdosing federal spending.

Indeed, increasing EV purchases would be far more effective if a viable infrastructure were already set in place. Sure, I might be tempted to buy an electric vehicle, given the tax credit, but would I actually drive it? If I want to drive from Troy to Chicago, will there be enough recharging stations? What happens if I get stuck? Would I be able to return? So how is this reducing inflation? In fact, EVs are on average more expensive. If anything, this tends to add to inflation because by increasing the demand for anything (without a concomitant increase in supply) its price will increase.

3) Reduce the cost of Medicare prescription drugs

This has long been a goal of the Democratic Left, and the pharmaceutical companies present a tempting target, notwithstanding that the Democrats ignore that a substantial lead time and cost is involved in bringing any new drug to market. Initially, the IRA will focus only on ten drugs (to begin in 2026), with an additional ten more subject to taxation in 2030. The IRA policy applies only to seniors (those over the age of sixty-five) already receiving Medicare and does not apply to anyone under the age of sixty-five purchasing such drugs. The IRA will impose a 95 percent penalty tax on firms that increase prices at a rate greater than the inflation rate. While this is another populist program attempting to assuage Americans that the administration has inflation under control, it has two major problems.

The first problem, the Biden administration is not using common sense. If you were told that your income would be significantly reduced in four years, would you sit idle and let come what may? Of course not! You would do whatever you could to raise prices now. In today's inflation environment, everyone is raising prices. The media is constantly talking about it. We have incentivized them to raise their prices now since they will not be able to do so in the future. This is like lighting a fire.

The second problem is that the IRA assumes a simplistic picture of the causes of inflation. While most economists assume that the causal factors of inflation are complex and multifaceted (emphasizing a strong relationship between the amount of money vis-à-vis the number of goods), the IRA assumes that inflation is caused by higher prescription prices, so by reducing drug prices we reduce inflation. Of course, increasing drug prices influences inflation, but it is certainly not the only cause—and to insist otherwise is disingenuous, dishonest, and counter-productive.

The US pharmaceutical industry is the most productive in the world. One reason they spend large amounts of money in the early stages of investment and research and development is the prospect of a greater return. Without this, they would be unwilling to spend and invest, and who knows what would be offered to the consumers. Sure, developing a drug takes years, and perhaps the FDA can expedite developing needed drugs quicker and more cheaply, but to tax pharmaceutical companies now, while America is on the cusp of recession and COVID still lingers is the wrong policy for the wrong time. We must continue to incentivize the pharmaceutical companies to do what they do best and not reduce their rate of return (as the Democrats insist) as a way of punishing them.

4) Phase out fossil fuels

Given Joe Manchin's preponderant role in the final bill, it should be no surprise that there are rewards for fossil fuel companies, given that his state (West Virginia) is a leading producer of fossil fuels. Yet at the same time there are significant penalties to the industry which in turn will increase inflation. So, what gives? Where and what is the underlying logic? This is an attempt to appease the fossil fuel states *and* the advocates of renewable energy within the Democratic Party:

- The IRA raises the superfund tax on crude oil and imported oil to 16.4 cents per barrel while increasing other taxes and fees on the fossil fuel sector. This will increase prices. How does this reduce inflation?

- The IRA has implemented the first nationwide tax on a global warming gas—methane—which is eighty times more powerful in trapping atmospheric heat than CO_2. Beginning in 2024, the IRA will impose a tax of $900/ton on methane emitted by oil and gas companies from wells, pipelines, LNG terminals, and other facilities. In 2026 the fee will increase to $1,500/ton.[36] But by increasing costs this will also increase inflation, while not doing anything to ease our current supply-side shortages.

Where is the wisdom of raising energy taxes in the middle of a recession and in the middle of an energy crisis?[37] Does the Biden administration have a personal vendetta against the oil and gas industries?

What the IRA will not do?

It is interesting that this act was not named the Medicare Price Reduction Act or the Electric Utility Vehicle Stimulus Act but the Inflation Reduction Act. Given its purported purpose and misleading name, we should be asking what the act will not (and cannot) do.

First and foremost, it will *not* reduce inflation. In fact, by increasing taxes on energy producers, incentivizing people to buy more EVs, and motivating pharmaceutical companies to increase prices now, the IRA can only increase inflation.

Not only will the IRA *not* reduce inflation in either the short run or long run, according to the Tax Foundation its long-run effects on the economy will be quite harmful:

- The IRA will reduce America's capital stock by 0.3 percent and wages by 0.1 percent, largely due to the 15 percent corporate tax and the tax on stock repurchases.

- For the same reason, the IRA decreases long-run economic growth (GDP) by 0.2 percent.

- It eliminates 29,000 full-time jobs (20,000 due to the corporate tax; 5,000 due to increasing Superfund taxes; and 7,000 due to the 1 percent excise tax on stock repurchases).

- It reduces after-tax incomes for American taxpayers across every income quintile. By so doing, it increases taxes on work and investment, and decreases productive activity.[38]

Given that the effect of the IRA is to contract the economy, it will increase inflation, all else equal, as the Tax Foundation explicitly warns: "By reducing long-run economic growth, this bill may actually worsen inflation by constraining the productive capacity of the economy."[39]

Looking at the Tax Foundation numbers you might say why the big deal? They aren't really that large: 25,000 jobs lost in a labor force of 165 million people, so why the alarm? But why settle for negative mediocrity, when my Two-Cents plan can actively expand growth by incentivizing Americans to produce more, achieve energy independence and decrease long-run inflation? Why settle for a policy that is deliberately misnamed, that will do the opposite of its intention?

In contrast, my Two-Cents plan policies will do exactly as intended. No gimmicks, no misleading false names, no deliberately tricking the American public, just common sense, and a refreshing dose of much-needed honesty.

Speaking of honesty, we need to briefly discuss Biden's executive order to reduce the student loan debt, given Biden claims that it is legally based on the IRA.

The Skyrocketing Cost of Education

An inflation reduction act should really look at the exorbitant rise in the cost of education. We all know that we have had dramatic increases in the cost of medical care which in most cases companies cannot afford to cover the total premium on medical benefits. While these increases have been outrageous, they are nothing compared to the staggering increase in the cost of education at the university level.

While increasing tuition has worried Americans since the early twentieth century, "the scale of these worries is [eye-popping] new."[40] Since the middle of the 1960s, tuition at our colleges and universities has been increasing at a rate far greater than inflation—and, in fact, more than any other product. Part of the reason for this may be due to the government getting involved in helping to finance education. In 1965 the Federal Family Education Loan (FFEL) program was enacted. The problem with this is that it was encumbering the incoming students with a tremendous burden. The government guaranteed these loans and put the students in a position where this debt could never be recused, not even through bankruptcy. The loan rates were set at 4.99 percent. Keep in mind when someone is seventeen or eighteen, they are not accustomed to having to pay back these large sums of money, and they have no idea of the ramifications. Not infrequently a student may end up with a degree in a field which does not enable them to have employment in that field. Hence, they are not able to repay these loans. Often the real world is not what they think it is at the age of seventeen or eighteen before going to college. For example, two people that work for Perry Johnson Mortgage Company, Inc. have master's degrees in sports management. They could not get jobs in sports management when they graduated and are saddled with this incredible debt that cannot be forgiven, even through bankruptcy. This is unreasonable.

Let's look at some numbers. In 1966, the year following the passage of this program, Harvard University tuition was $1,352, while today it is $52,659.[41] An increase of 3,795 percent! If the tuition increases had merely kept pace with inflation, then tuition would only be $12,438 today.[42]

These startling numbers are in the same neighborhood as other private colleges and universities, but of course substantially higher than public schools, such as the nearby University of Massachusetts-Amherst, the state's flagship public university. In 1966, the tuition and fees at UMass Amherst were $375.00. Today the tuition and fees are $16,952 for in-state residents.[43] That is an increase of 4,500 percent, even more than Harvard University. If it increased only at the rate of inflation the cost today for Amherst college the tuition today would be only $3,450.00 approximately one-fifth of what it is today.

In addition to worrying about higher gas and energy prices, interest rates, mortgage rates and all of that, I'm sure today's students, somewhere in the back of their minds, are worried about the cost of tuition when their children are ready to go to college. Once again, let's use Harvard University as our example. If we assume (quite reasonably) that tuition will continue to increase at a 6.3 percent annual clip, then in thirty years, when the children of today's students are ready to enroll, tuition for one year at Harvard will cost an astronomical $329,208. Compare this to $52,659 now. If we add room and board, the total cost for one year at Harvard will be $463,876. Yikes! Keep in mind gas prices in 1966 were .29 cents per gallon. If prices had gone up at the same rate as college tuition, we would now be paying $9.88 per gallon! To put it in perspective the current median income for a family of four is $70,784.00.[44] In 1966 the median income for a family of four was $7,400.00.[45] If our incomes had increased at the same rate as college tuition (6.3 percent) the median family income in the United States would be $213,089.00, over three times what it is today. It is important to know that other countries have not increased tuition at anywhere near the rate of the United States. For example, at Oxford University the cost for tuition is £9,250 per year, which is equivalent to $10,872.00.

These numbers are eye popping and enough to cripple any middle-class family. But where is the outcry, the clarion call to do something to stop this? Where is the concern of the Biden administration?

Cartoon 10 – College Kids Talking

Should we be concerned?

At the expense of stating the obvious, yes, of course, we should be concerned:

- For our nation to grow we need educated workers and citizens. This in the only way to increase our productivity and our standard of living. We look to our colleges, universities, and two-year schools as the primary way of doing so.

- The law of demand, a basic law of economics, states that as the price of anything increases the quantity demanded will decrease, ceteris paribus. So, as college tuition increases, we can expect more potential students will be excluded from pursuing a college education, which in turn will drag down our productivity.

- Partly due to increasing tuition, the amount of student loan debt has increased nine-fold since 1995, from $187 billion to $1.7 trillion, and shows no signs of slowing down.[46] In fact, given the ease of obtaining loans, colleges and universities feel that they can increase tuition at will, since students will increasingly borrow. The upward spiral continues.

It is for these reasons that "college tuition is therefore both a public policy for the country, and a personal issue for the students."[47]

So, what's going on?

As a young man, Adam Smith, the founder of economics, attended Oxford University. Back then, as today, its stellar reputation attracted the best and brightest. Smith, however, was very critical of the poor quality of teaching, even noting in the *Wealth of Nations* that in the University of Oxford, "the greater part of the professors, have, for these many years, given up all together even the pretense of teaching."[48] On the other hand, Smith, was quite favorable toward his own Scottish universities. The main difference between the two was that in Scottish universities, students paid their professors directly based on the quality of the instruction and how much they learned. Whereas at Oxford the student paid a general fee to the University which in turn, the University distributed as it saw fit, while paying the professor a set salary. Thus,

> In Smith's universities there was a better alignment between value obtained and cost willingly paid. [After all] Prices are information about what people need and want, so the trouble with bundling together a large number of services on a single bill is that it becomes difficult to tell exactly what one is paying for, or for the people sending out that bill to determine what students in fact want to pay for.[49]

Today's colleges compete for students in several different ways: intellectual quality of its programs and professors, job placement ability, and amenities like student centers, intramural facilities, dining halls, dorms, food services, and intercollegiate sports stadiums.

Indeed, with all this extra spending, one might naturally wonder how much money from tuition actually goes toward actual instruction. If you guessed less than one-third, you get a cigar.

In 2019-2020, averaging across all four-year schools, public and private, 30.1 percent of total expenditures was devoted to instruction, down slightly from 32.4 percent in 1980, the earliest year that I could get comprehensive data.[50] Since 1980, academic support has increased (from 6.7 percent to 8.71 percent of total expenditures); student services have increased from 4.5 percent to 8.26 percent; institutional support from 9.0 percent to 12.45 percent, and hospitals from 8.5 percent to 14.75 percent. The latter the biggest gainer since 1980.[51]

Of course, I do not intend to disparage the work of any of these ancillary services, for the evidence indicates that they increase both the retention rate and the graduation rate, as well as overall well-being. But my point is that the link between cost paid, and value obtained has long been de-coupled. This is the same problem that Adam Smith wrote about in the *Wealth of Nations*. Students are forced to pay for a plethora of services they may or may not use, while professors have no direct say in how their product is priced and offered directly to students.

Today's government leaders fail to see the depth and the complexity of the problem. They have failed to take adequate action to arrest the underlying causes. Dealing with the causes of spiraling tuition and finding an equitable and workable solution for all is by no means easy. Dealing with the cost of a spiraling tuition is particularly burdensome on the student and the parents. We need a broad-based discussion. This is what we do in a democracy: Talk and dialogue and work out an equitable solution for all.

To get the ball rolling I propose adding a college student to the Cabinet. Yes, I am serious. Here are my reasons: (1) such a position would provide valuable insight into working through the complex and multifaceted causes of our spiraling tuition and to provide a workable solution; (2) any well-functioning economy, in addition to enabling its current citizens to adequately provision, should also lay the foundation for the next generation to adequately provision for itself. Too often we forget this. Why not hear directly from students, the leaders of our next generation? But this is what capitalism is all about.

I look forward to dialoguing with students across this great country of ours on how best to solve this problem of spiraling tuition. I suggest that my Two-Cents plan policy apply to the colleges and universities as well and they look at decreasing the budget instead of increasing the budget each year. Let's face it only 30 percent of the money they are collecting is even going to the professors. Does cutting 2 percent off the budget each year sound all that unreasonable if we are to prevent our students from being saddled with these unreasonable burdens?

The Exploding Cost of Medical

A few years ago, I received a flyer in the mail that they were offering a special on a whole-body scan for $99. I took advantage of this offer. The scan took about forty minutes, and they gave me a disk immediately afterwards. They also arranged a time for me to speak with the radiologist over the phone. I was delighted when he told me that everything looked great. One of my best friends is a radiologist. I gave him the disk; he slipped it into the computer, and we looked at it together. I found it quite fascinating. Subsequently, I found out that if I had this done in the hospital the price would have been several thousand dollars.

In the United States we have the most bizarre pricing for medical procedures that often has no rhyme or reason. It may be hard to believe but the hospital would actually charge you based on whether you were paying cash or whether you were insured. What is even more ridiculous is that even the insurance companies have different amounts that they pay for the same procedure. Price disclosures at some Los Angeles hospitals demonstrate that prices regularly vary.

Figure 2.5 Price Comparisons for Standard Noncontrast Brain MRI at
L.A. Area Hospitals

Price Comparisons for Standard Noncontrast Brain MRI (CPT CODE: 70551) at LA-Area Hospitals				
	Cedars–Sinai Medical Center		Pomona Valley Hospital Medical Center	
Aetna PPO	$	2,964	$	2,427
Blue Cross HMO	$	2,162		
Blue Cross Sr HMO	$	367		
Blue Shield HMO	$	2,664	$	5,646
Blue Shield PPO	$	2,664	$	5,646
Cigna PPO	$	3,245	$	6,500
Healthnet HMO	$	3,540	$	6,766
Healthnet PPO	$	3,540	$	6,766
Kaiser	$	4,043		
UHC_HMO	$	2,079	$	1,210
UHC_PPO	$	2,702	$	1,283
Medi-Cal HealthCare LA				
Cash			$	450

Blanks reflect lack of payer price published by hospital
Source: Cedars-Sinai, Torrance Memorial, Huntington Hospital, and Pomona Valley hospital pricing website pages:
https://www.cedars-sinai.org/billing-insurance.html
https://www.pvhmc.org/documents/insurance-Combined-List-2021-12.txt

At the Pomona Valley Hospital Medical Center if you do a standard non-contrast brain MRI , and you have a Healthnet HMO the cost is $6,766. If you pay cash, it is $450. What is amazing is that if you are like most people that have to pay 20 percent out of the first $5,000, it would cost you twice as much than if you had no insurance at all. Keep in mind that the hospital is getting an additional $5,000.00 from the insurance company. That means it is over 1,200 percent more for the same procedure if you have insurance!

What has happened to the health care system over the last fifty years is shocking. The prices in the United States have gone up more than any other place in the world and yet we have done worse in life expectancy than other developed countries. It is important to note that in 1970 life expectancy in America was one and a half years greater than the average life expectancy in the Organization for Economic Cooperation and Development, or OECD, countries (the thirty-eight well-developed countries)[.52]

Cartoon 11 – Comparing the Cost of MRI Scans

Our cost for medical care at that time was greater than the other members of the OECD, but it was only 1.5 percent of gross domestic product greater. Now our life expectancy is 2.9 years less than the average of the members of the OECD, despite the fact that our health care costs have soared relative to the rest of the world. Our medical costs now are 10.5 percent of our gross domestic product, greater than the other members of the OECD. Compared to 1970 the United States has declined 4.4 years in life expectancy when compared to the average change in life expectancy of the other countries in the OECD. Yet if we look at our cost relative to gross domestic product, we are 700 percent greater if we use that as a benchmark for relative cost. The cost for medical care in the United States is 16.8 percent of gross domestic product in the United States as of 2019. The country with the next highest medical care costs is Germany at 11.7 percent of gross domestic product. Switzerland is number three in cost with medical care cost at 11.3 percent of gross domestic product. Keep in mind that both of those countries are doing better than the US in terms of life expectancy. Germany's life expectancy is 81.4 years and Switzerland is 84 years. This is compared to the United States which is only 78.9 years.[53]

While I started Perry Johnson, Inc., in 1983, I did not provide insurance to the employees until 1986. At that time, I covered the insurance for the employees, and the total cost was about $18.00 per month. I don't remember the exact coverage, but there was virtually no out of pocket expenditures on the part of the insured. Today the coverage for an individual in my company with the least expensive policy is $577.56 per month. There is a potential out-of-pocket expenditure of $2,500 per year plus an additional $1,000 per year copay for prescription drugs. It is worse coverage than in 1986, and yet the rates have increased 3,208 percent! Had health insurance cost increased at the rate of inflation it would cost $49.16 per month today and not $577.56.

Annual premiums for a family of three with employer-sponsored health insurance averaged $22,221 annually ($1,851.75 per month), according to the 2021 benchmark KFF Employer Health Benefits Survey. Keep in mind this does not include copays or co-insurance payments, which may not be included in their plan. In 2020 health care spending in the United States was over $4,000.00 per person more expensive than any other high-income country. The average amount spent on health per person in comparable countries was $5,736.00, approximately half what the health care spending was per person in the United States.[54]

Figure 2.6 Health Consumption Expenditures Per Capita, U.S. Dollars

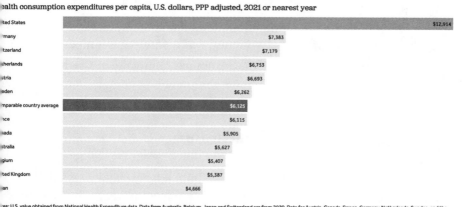

ealth consumption expenditures per capita, U.S. dollars, PPP adjusted, 2021 or nearest year

ited States	$12,914
rmany	$7,383
tzerland	$7,179
therlands	$6,753
stria	$6,693
eden	$6,262
mparable country average	$6,125
nce	$6,115
nada	$5,905
stralia	$5,627
gium	$5,407
ted Kingdom	$5,387
an	$4,666

es: U.S. value obtained from National Health Expenditure data. Data from Australia, Belgium, Japan and Switzerland are from 2020. Data for Austria, Canada, France, Germany, Netherlands, Sweden, and the ted Kingdom are provisional. Data from Canada represents a difference in methodology from the prior year. Health consumption does not include investments in structures, equipment, or research.

rce: KFF analysis of National Health Expenditure (NHE) and OECD data • Get the data • PNG

Peterson-KFF
Health System Tracker

The real cause of these escalating prices is that we do not have the natural competitive marketplace in play. It is extremely easy to spend somebody else's money, and even though we are really paying for it indirectly, in our minds it is covered by insurance. If we want to buy a house or a car, we would want to know the price before we bought it. But this is not happening with medical care at the hospitals. Obviously, it is imperative that we know how much we are spending if we are going to have any hope of trying to control cost. The best way for us to have a competitive force is by allowing insurance companies to quote across state lines. Then the companies and individuals will pay attention to the actual premium cost. The insurance companies will be forced to put pressure on all the hospitals and doctors to have a more consistent cost structure at lower prices. Keep in mind where insurance is not covering a procedure, such as Lasik eye surgery or elective plastic surgery, prices have actually come down relative to inflation over the last thirty years.

In order to achieve competition, it is obvious that we must have transparency of pricing. It should be necessary for every hospital and clinic to post the prices for every procedure. President Trump did sign an executive order relative to this, and this is one executive order that President Biden did not extinguish. Even Biden agreed on the importance of transparency in pricing. I believe that the hospitals and clinics should implement my Two-Cents policy. Interstate competition and transparent pricing will force the insurance companies to reduce their prices.

Conclusion

Thomas Piketty noted in his best-selling book *Capital in the Twenty-First Century* that in the eighteenth and nineteenth centuries, despite ephemeral periods of inflation and deflation, prices were overall quite stable, which went a long way toward comforting and re-assuring citizens. It was not until the delinking of paper money from gold (in part caused by the massive spending during WWI) and the widespread acceptance of central banks printing money at will (i.e., fiat money) that government spending and the money supply exploded.

Confidence is high that the Fed's policies will temporarily reduce demand-induced inflation by bludgeoning the economy to death. But given the role of fiscal mismanagement in the current inflation, traditional monetary policy is not enough.

> Not only fiscal inflation tends to be highly persistent, but it also requires a different policy response. When inflation has a fiscal nature, monetary policy alone may not provide an effective response... [and] the central bank is not uniquely responsible for its reduction... Conquering the post-pandemic inflation necessitates an overhaul of the fiscal framework aimed at financing the large stock of government debt as well as the increase in public expenditure needed to cover rising costs associated with population aging and climate change.[55]

This is exactly what my inflation-reducing policies will do.

After peaking at 9.1 percent in June 2022, the inflation rate fell to 8.3 percent in August, prompting cheers from the Biden camp that its anti-inflation policies and energy policies are working. Two comments here:

- The administration's anti-inflation policies are policies in name only, and perhaps "policies" is a misnomer since it suggests a logical and coherent plan, and not the mumbo jumbo we see almost on a daily basis from the administration.

- Why celebrate an inflation rate that has not been this high since the days of Jimmy Carter? Is the administration deliberately trying to evoke the memories of failed economic policies?

As *The Economist* reminds us, "America still has an inflation problem... which shows little sign of going away."[56] If we strip away volatile food and energy prices, *the core inflation rate*[57] actually rose at an annual rate of 7.4 percent in August 2022 and shows no signs of slowing down. This is mainly because the

> effects of generous fiscal stimulus, which stoked demand during the pandemic, linger today. According to Goldman Sachs… households in aggregate are still sitting on more than $2 trillion in excess saving accumulated during lockdowns, equivalent to 10 percent of annual GDP. And a tight labor market [at least right now] with a still [relatively 'low'] unemployment rate of 3.7 percent is boosting wages which in turn is boosting consumer demand."[58]

The stubborn persistence of the core inflation rate has my economist friends worried that the Fed will continue raising interest rates (i.e., its federal funds rate) for the duration of this year and into the early part of 2023.[59] Especially now that the Bureau of Labor Statistics reports that the USA unemployment dipped to 3.5 percent in September 2022, after increasing to 3.7 percent in August.

On the contrary, my Two-Cents policies offer a more humane (and more cohesive) set of inflation policies based on a better understanding of its underlying causes.

CHAPTER 3

Incentivizing America's Workers

As I am writing this chapter, three of my favorite restaurants are closed for lunch because of staff shortages. In my business I find it exceedingly difficult to find employees. My businessowner friends are in a similar situation. No one is able to get the staff that they need. Everywhere I turn I see help wanted signs. This is standard throughout our country. As of September 2022, American businesses have posted 10.1 million job openings.

MY TWO-CENTS PLAN
ON THE LABOR FORCE

Reverse current policies that disincentivize work, while actively promoting labor force participation.

But how can this be with an unemployment rate humming along at 3.5 percent. Surely this shortage is due to Covid. Haven't we all heard stories of burned-out doctors, teachers, and nurses quitting their jobs? Once the virus weakens and we are finally done with it, our economy will return to normal and anyone who wants to work can find a job, right?

That is not what is happening. Here is why.

The US Labor Force Participation Rate

The shortage of workers confronting the American economy predates COVID-19 and by all accounts will continue long afterward unless
something is done now. The labor force participation rate (LFPR) di-
vides those of us in the labor force (either employed or unemployed) by
those of us who are age-eligible to work (over the age of sixteen and
not in prison). The current labor force participation rate of 62 percent
means that for every 100 age-eligible Americans 62 are participating in
the labor force.[1] Put another way: 38 percent of us who could be working are not, a percentage that has been steadily increasing.

Figure 3.1 The USA labor force participation rate 1950- 2021

*https://www.bls.gov/opub/mlr/2013/article/labor-force-projections-to-2022-the-labor-force-
participation-rate-continues-to-fall.htm*

As Figure 3.2 illustrates, this decrease has occurred for both men and
women, although the trend has been more pronounced for men, which
is more problematic.[2]

Figure 3.2 The decline in the USA LFPR for men and women

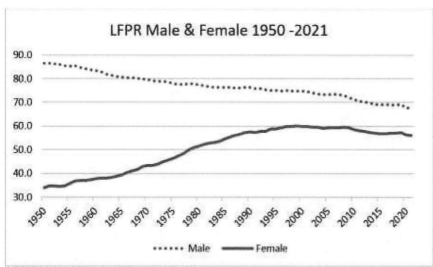

https://fred.stlouisfed.org/categories/32443

No one wants to live in an economy where everyone is working and no one is caring for children or sick relatives, or going to school or even in between jobs. But at the same time, we *do* expect that in a vibrant dynamic economy we will have enough workers to produce the goods and services we need.

But we have ourselves to blame for this troubling decline in the labor force. Or more technically correct, we can blame bad government policies that disincentivize the will to work. Why work if you can get something for free? Many people might ask themselves why work if you can make a living without lifting a finger?

That is how socialism worked (if *worked* is the right word). But look around, do you see any socialist nations still standing? For the few that are left, what are the living standards of their people? In America, or at least the America I have known (and would like to restore), we have always worked to obtain an income to buy the goods and services we need. By doing so, we feel good about actively participating in the economy. We buy homes, send our kids to school, and take active care and interest in our neighborhoods. But government handouts, whether they

pay workers not to work or give Americans gratuitous stimuli, attenuate the connection between work and income. It also makes us feel
less good about ourselves and America.[3]

But Americans should never have been incentivized *not* to work. It
is about time that our government stops enabling. My Two-Cents policies will reverse this deplorable situation. By doing so, my policies will
help America get back on the right track.

Reform the Americans with Disabilities Act

In 1930, inactive men (not working or looking for work) comprised
only 2 percent of males between the ages of 25 and 54. This percentage
has since increased to 11 percent today. Inactive men have fewer skills,
live in poorer homes and neighborhoods, and have poor physical or
mental health. Two-thirds of today's inactive men receive government
assistance, while one-third have criminal records.[4]

Cartoon 12 – Hammock Employment

The decline in the LFPR of male prime workers is heavily concentrated among those with a high school education or less. Interestingly, given their low wages, the opportunity cost of not working is lower. In other words, since a worker earning, let's say, $20,000 per year sacrifices a lot less to drop out of the labor force than a person earning $100,000 per year, the latter would be less willing to drop out, all else equal, than the former, since the opportunity cost (i.e., missed income) of foregoing $100,000 is a lot more than the opportunity cost of foregoing $20,000.

A recent (and authoritative) Federal Reserve study, found that prime-aged men have dropped out of the labor force for the following reasons:

- Early retirement (10 percent)

- Returning to school (10 percent)

- Staying at home to raise children or care for a sick relative (15 percent)

- Becoming discouraged (12 percent), i.e., giving up the search for work, convinced that there isn't anything available

- Claiming a disability (43 percent)

- Other (10 percent)[5]

In 1990 Congress passed The Americans with Disabilities Act (ADA).[6] The Act has two primary objectives: (1) it is unlawful to discriminate in employment against a qualified individual with a disability;[7] and (2) it makes more resources available for disability and expands the disability definition to include depression and mental health.

Let's zoom in on the last reason, claiming a disability, and take a look at how that affected the number of people in America on disability.

Figure 3.3 Americans with a disability

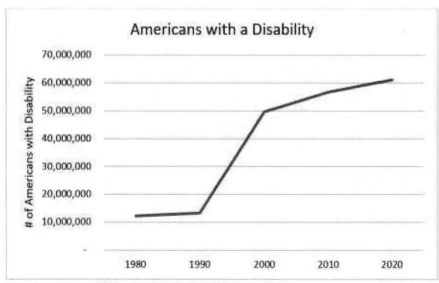

Source: CDC, https://files.eric.ed.gov/fulltext/ED282370.pdf

All government legislation creates unintended consequences (or dis-incentives if you will). A good example is unemployment compensation, which theoretically provides a cushion for laid-off workers in search of work. The more generous the cushion, the more likely the period of searching will be increased, ironically increasing the unemployment rate. Yes, we want to help the unemployed get back on their feet by aligning their skills with what is available, which, by the way is in the best interests of society. But at the same time, we do not want to offer benefits generous enough to discourage the unemployed from diligently searching. In other words, we do not want to disincentivize the incentives.

The ADA emphatically states that to receive benefits, one must demonstrate an inability to perform work.[8] More specifically, the Social Security Administration notes that "No benefits are payable for partial disability or for short-term disability." Just to make sure that there is no ambiguity, the Social Security Administration states emphatically that "we consider you to have a qualifying disability under Social Security rules if all the following are true:

- You cannot do work and engage in substantial gainful activity (SGA) because of your medical condition.

- You cannot do work you did previously or adjust to other work because of your medical condition.

- Your condition has lasted or is expected to last for at least one year or to result in death."

Cartoon 13 – Something to Cheer About

An obviously strong work disincentive. While the evidence isn't 100 percent conclusive (when is it ever?) the preponderance of evidence suggests that a direct relationship exists between the ADA and males dropping out of the labor force. Terry Jones of Investor's Business Daily writes:

The Americans with Disabilities Act, passed in 1990, greatly expanded the definition of who's disabled. It also boosted financial and other resources for them. So, many Americans with limitations who would have kept working in a prior era because they had nochoice now have a choice: keep working or go on disability. For those living in pain as they struggle from paycheck to paycheck, disability is often the clear choice.[9]

But don't blame workers for doing something in their best interest. Blame the policymakers for designing such a system with a deliberate disincentive to work.

In crafting any solution, it is important to distinguish between individuals who can work and those who cannot. Of course, this doesn't mean that one must necessarily work in the same job or even the same industry. Certainly, in today's changing economy, workers must be able to adapt to shifting wants and needs. After all, businesses must be dynamic and adapt or they become extinct.

Fortunately, we can look to both the Earned Income Tax Credit (EITC), established in 1975, and the 1996 Personal Responsibility and Work Opportunity Reconciliation Act (PRWORA)—also known as the Welfare Reform Act—as good working role models. The EITC, a favorite of Milton Freidman, and a favorite of mine, eliminates income taxes completely via tax credits for low-income workers. The tax credit is gradually phased out as income increases, and in doing so, maintains an incentive to work. Currently the minimum age to participate in the EITC is twenty-five, but there is no reason why the age cannot be lowered to sixteen, while also doubling the maximum credit and expanding the income range, which in turn will increase the labor force participation rate. The EITC should be applied to all individuals regardless of whether they have children. The goal of my Two-Cents plan is to incentivize people to work and reward them accordingly.

The Temporary Assistance for Needy Families (TANF), which replaced the Aid to Families with Dependent Children, calls for all recipients to work after receiving benefits for two years. One can meet the work provision by employment, performing community service, or vocational training. In addition, the TANF places a five-year maximum on receiving benefits.

The consensus among economists is that both the EITC and the PRWORA, while certainly not perfect, have achieved their objectives: reducing welfare and incentivizing work for the latter—and maintaining the incentive to work for low-income households for the former. So why not apply these same principles to the ADA?

We can start by borrowing from the specific words or phrases of the EITC, the PRWORA, and the TANF: *temporary, assistance, Personal Responsibility, Work Opportunity,* are all positive forward-looking words or phrases that incentivize and enable hammering home the message of what these policies are all about. Compare this with the stigmatizing *Americans with Disabilities* phrase that says, "I am an American, and I cannot work because I am disabled." Perhaps a more motivating name would be the Work Opportunities Act. Then:

- Replace the criteria that one must demonstrate an inability to work with ascertaining how and where every disabled individual can and might work. Both the worker and the firm could look toward remote work, and if not immediately available, look for a mutually beneficial solution.

- Require that all ADA recipients, after two years of receiving benefits, either to work or obtain vocational training with the goal of eventually landing a job. This is not to say that the individual returns to his or her industry or occupation but rather investigates possible jobs that exist for those who are disabled. This will motivate individuals to receive necessary treatments and employment training as well.

- Mandate that disability payments can be received for a maximum total of only five years. Of course, our goal is not to callously jettison all assistance, especially for those who absolutely cannot work, but to incentivize those who can work while providing a cushion for those who cannot. The Social Security Disability Program (SSDI) and/or Medicaid can help the disabled who are truly unable to work. Why lump all disabled Americans together as if they can never work again?

- Our government (at all levels) should work with local business groups and chambers of commerce to help get more disabled Americans into the workplace. The opportunity for work should not just be the responsibility of the individual. Businesses should be incentivized to make their workplaces and their jobs amenable for the disabled. Modern technology means jobs can often come to the worker rather than the worker going to the job.

Work Incentivize Medicaid

Medicaid and Medicare (created in 1965) provide health care insurance for the needy.[10] In a much-cited study, the Kaiser Family Foundation estimated that among Medicaid recipients there are 1 million non-elderly, non-disabled people without a good reason to be jobless.[11] Incentivizing these people to work by using the lessons from the EITC and TANF could increase the overall LFPR by 1 percent. Of course, it is important not to put people into any job but to find the right job for the right person. It is important to carefully distinguish between those able to work and those not able to do so.

Tackle the Opioid Crisis

Close to half of all inactive prime-age men take pain medication daily, with two-thirds using prescription-based medications.[12] Of these prescription-based medications, opioids have received the most attention. Since 1999 almost one million Americans have died from opioids, a tragic loss of life. It is America's deadliest-ever drug crisis.

Figure 3.4 The USA opioid death rate

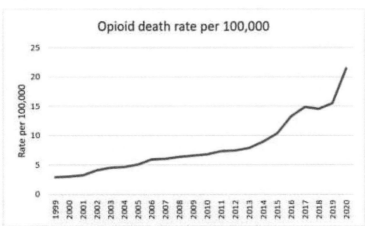

Source: https://www.kff.org/other/state-indicator/opioid-overdose-death-
rates/?activeTab=graph&currentTimeframe=0&startTimeframe=21&selectedRows=%7B%22wra
pups%22:%7B%22unitedstates%22:%7B%7D%7D%7D&sortModel=%7B%22colId%22:%22Locatio
n%22,%22sort%22:%22asc%22%7D

In a widely quoted study, Alan Krueger of Princeton University found that the increase in opioid prescriptions from 1999 to 2015 could account for 43 percent of the observed decline in men's labor force participation during that same period.[13]

Opioids, while legal, are prescribed for pain medication, but given their high addictiveness, once the prescription expires, an individual often seeks other illicit substances that are even more addictive. The logical solution is to reduce opioid prescriptions and reduce or eliminate the importation of opioids of all types into the USA.

In February of 2022, the major drug distributors Cardinal Health, McKesson, and AmerisourceBergen and drugmaker Johnson & Johnson agreed to provide $26 billion for remediation of the opioid epidemic in exchange for states dropping future legal claims against them. Johnson & Johnson agreed to pay $5 billion over a maximum of nine years, and the drug distributors agreed to pay $21 billion over eighteen years, with 70 percent of the settlement money earmarked for future opioid remediation efforts, including intervention, treatment, education, and recovery services. Surely there must be a natural remedy or something non-addictive to prescribe?[14]

By the way, we should be restricting the flow of illegal drugs, just as we should be disincentivizing illegal immigrants from trying to enter the USA (More on this in Chapter 5).

Facilitate the opportunity of incarcerated individuals to return to the labor force.

Since 1980 the American incarceration rate has increased fivefold. Since this stigmatizes the individual and makes it more difficult to obtain a job after release, this dramatic increase has significantly reduced the male LFPR. The National Conference of State Legislatures tells us that prison labor barriers (e.g., stigma, direct prohibition, lack of effective skills, etc.) account for a loss of 1.7 million employees, or about a one percentage point in the LFPR, at a cost of at least $78 billion to the economy.[15]

Some people—especially crime victims—might argue that offenders should be locked away for good, without any chance for release, never mind rehabilitation. While emotionally we might think this "tough on crime" approach is good, the essence of a democracy is a fair and just penalty for a crime, and a chance for rehabilitation. Unless our societal goal is to lock up every prisoner for life, which, by the way, we cannot justify either ethically or financially, then we must ease the transition of formerly incarcerated individuals into the labor force while not ignoring the role that stiff prison sentences play in lessening the incentive to commit a crime. This is what law and order is all about.

Given our 10.1 million job openings, the business community has become more amenable to hiring incarcerated individuals. In a 2021 survey by the Society for Human Resource Management and the Charles Koch Institute, 53 percent of HR professionals said they would be willing to hire people with criminal records, up from 37 percent in 2018.

The crux of our justice system is that the criminals must pay their debt to society. Fair enough. But part of the debt should be effective rehabilitation to equip them to reenter the labor force as long as they pose no threats to others. A condition for release should be that inmates learn basic work skills and a specific trade. If an individual refuses, then no release; and if they agree, welcome to the labor force.

We want to create an environment so that when inmates get out of prison, they have a good chance at a reasonable life without returning to crime. We must help facilitate that. We must create an environment where individuals from all walks of life can succeed. This requires equipping people with the right incentives to want to work more and to keep and enjoy the proceeds from doing so.

Although not everyone is keen on hiring a former convict, it is a necessary step in providing hope and rehabilitating self-esteem, while recognizing that keeping every convict locked up for good will bankrupt our budget. Yes, of course, let us keep the incorrigible and hopelessly violent locked up. Studies indicate that a steady *good* job is the best guarantee against recidivism, and by reducing recidivism, we also reduce the costs to society, both in the short and long term. Jennifer Doleac of Texas A&M writes that

> Two-thirds of those released from prison are arrested again within three years. Breaking this incarceration cycle is a top policy priority, but it is unclear which programs are effective at achieving this goal. Those who are employed are less likely to reoffend, and this correlation has led many to think that increasing access to jobs could be the key to reducing recidivism.[16]

But as Doleac notes, the specifics of how to do this most efficiently is not clear. A lot of variables must be effectively considered. Sifting through the evidence she concludes: A key takeaway of those studies is that access to *good* jobs—not just any jobs—reduces recidivism. That is, only jobs in industries that pay well, such as construction, seem to be effective.[17]

Incentivize our older workers to continue to work.

Thanks to innovative medical technology, and the continuous development of life-saving drugs, Americans are living longer. In 1940, average life expectancy at birth was an overall 62.9 years, with men living to 60.8 and women to 62.9. Since then, it has steadily increased, until COVID. From 2020 to 2021 overall life expectancy at birth dropped from 77.0 years to 76.1 years, which came on the heels of a 1.8 year drop in life expectancy in 2020, making that the largest two-year decrease since 1921-1923. From 2020 to 2021, life expectancy at birth for women decreased from 79.9 years to 79.1, and for men 74.2 to 73.2 years.[18]

When Social Security was first introduced in 1935, life expectancy for a male (in a male-dominated labor force and a male-dominated economy) was 59.3 years. But today, with a more diverse labor force people are living longer and hence need to work. People are physically stronger, mentally more acute, and in much better physical shape. We have to incentivize people to want to work.

In a vibrant dynamic capitalistic economy, one needs to work to feel economically franchised, to feel like one is contributing to our economy while providing for one's family. This is the American Dream.

While the benefits of staying in the labor force largely depend on a job's specific characteristics, the overall evidence suggests that working (and working longer) is beneficial. This is largely due to the positive effects of social networking and continued activation of the brain; while, at the same time, work gives individuals a purpose, a routine, a reason for getting up in the morning.

Work offers a routine and purpose, a reason for getting up in the morning. The workplace is a social environment, a community.

Depending on your occupation, doing your job involves engaging with cubicle mates, bosses, subordinates, union brothers and sisters, suppliers, vendors and customers. The incentive for workers to invest in their health while employed is strong.[19]

Interestingly, workers who retire early and are lucky to earn a pension, such as police and fire fighters, will sometimes, instead of leaving the labor force, dabble in a part-time, low-wage job such as fast food or mall security. In so doing, they compete with teens, especially those not enrolled in school, reinforcing the wage gap between educated and non-educated workers. Maybe such workers can be rehired at the entry wage by their department while still retaining their pension? It would be cheaper, while at the same time not crowding out teenage employment, especially those not enrolled in school.

Conversely, the effects of not working or losing one's job are well documented: higher divorce rates, alcoholism, spousal abuse, depression, loss of self-esteem. These effects can, in turn, wreak havoc on family and community life. If a job is fulfilling and the working environment positive, then the documented benefits of working (and for older workers, working more) are myriad: lower blood pressure, lower risk of stroke, a better immune system, lower risk of cardiovascular disease, lower depression, and less anxiety.[20] Work makes people happier and gives them a greater zest for life.

There is no reason why a healthy older person should not continue to work as long as he or she is able and willing. My grandfather, who grew up in Johnstown, Pennsylvania, put his own roof on when he was ninety-three! I remember visiting him one afternoon, and while chatting, he said that one of his friends was thinking of retiring at the age of seventy. "I don't understand why he would do something like this," my grandfather told me. "He is in the prime of life." In reality people are living longer, and they are healthier than they ever were. Let us not forget that the average life expectancy was sixty when people were retiring at sixty-five, and now the average life expectancy in the United States is around seventy-eight.

The policy of the federal government should be to incentivize work while ensuring that incentives do not degenerate into disincentives. Gabriel Heller-Sahlgreen, of the Center for the Study of Market Reform of Education, adds, "This does not mean that politicians should force people to work until they die. They should [however] remove the disincentives to working."[21]

Emphasize the Trades

Schools should actively teach the trades rather than focus exclusively on a college track. Currently, in the USA, 38 percent of women and 33 percent of men have a college degree.[22]

These numbers, and the gap between men and women with college degrees, are expected to increase. Incidentally, more educated women delay childbirth, have fewer children, are more likely to use daycare services, and participate more in the labor force than less-educated women.[23]

There are several drivers in this increasing trend of more college graduates:

- A significant and growing wage gap between university/college graduates and non-university graduates. In 2020, the median weekly wage of a high school graduate was $781; with a bachelor's degree $1,305, and with a professional degree, $1,893.[24]

- Well-recognized non-benefits of a university education such as better access to more meaningful jobs, greater health, lower rates of disability, greater longevity, and greater satisfaction with one's work and one's life.[25]

- A lack of emphasis on the well-paying jobs available for non-college graduates. College is not for everyone, and we certainly do not want to live in a nation where everyone attends college, and no one practices any of the trades. In high school, students are seldom taught the earning potential of various trades vis-à-vis the jobs readily available for university graduates. A journeyman electrician, for example, will make $27 an hour right out of the gate. This does not account for overtime, nor the possibility of becoming a skilled subcontractor, or even owning one's business—a common pathway for the construction trades, where incomes could top $250,000 to $300,000 per year. Tom Leonard, a friend of mine from college, got a degree in accounting. During the summers he worked as a carpenter. Ironically, with a degree in accounting, he would not earn as much money as he would as a journeyman carpenter. Granted, back then the construction industry was booming—this was the 1970s—and he worked sizable overtime. Another example: at a friend's birthday party, I sat next to a man who introduced himself as Bill. He modestly said that he had decided to build single family homes. It was interesting for me to hear his life story since at the time I was a young entrepreneur. I later learned that his name was Pulte, and many of us are familiar with his multi-million-dollar construction business, which is listed on the NYSE.

- Working at a trade is an admirable (and relatively lucrative) way to make a living and should be part of a solid track for those who do not want to attend college. According to the BLS, "about 60 percent of new jobs in the economy generated between 2020 and 2030 will be in occupations that do not typically require an associate's, bachelor's, or graduate degree.[26] A few such examples: wind turbine service technicians (with a median annual wage of $56,260), aircraft mechanics ($65,380), millwrights ($60,330), subway/streetcar operators ($81,180), and industrial machinery mechanics ($59,840).

The USA lacks a focus on educating our students for the trades and for a non-college track. My policies will reverse this neglect. Doing so will not only provide meaningful jobs for a significant sector of our society, but it will also boost productivity and strengthen our economy.

Any dynamic economy will always have a mismatch between the skills needed and the existing skills of the members of the labor force. The more dynamic the economy the greater this mismatch. I am sure none of us would welcome the alternative: a stationary, non-growing, non-innovating economy (much like existed in the Middle Ages, or in the old USSR, or in any socialist nation).

The problem is that our apprenticeship programs train workers for the current skills demanded, rather than on how the labor market functions and how to look for work and possibly retrain if one loses one's job. Workers, if they are laid off and are told that their skills are no longer needed by either their company or their industry, often do not have the resources to train, nor do they know exactly that for which to train. This is a main reason why workers become discouraged.

Secondary schools require math, science, English, social studies, and computer science. Shouldn't we have some focus on getting people introduced to basic job skills, maybe even entrepreneurship? In that way we could indoctrinate them into the importance of understanding the basics of the economy and its dynamic nature. They may also learn that the skills from today may not be the skills needed tomorrow. That education is critical in learning how to adapt, which, of course, requires a different set of skills. So, in addition to teaching specific trades, high schools should teach how to learn, how to improvise, and how to self-provision—all necessary skills in today's economy. Such a class could even be taught by an older individual looking to reenter the labor force.

Conclusion

A price to pay for living in the world's most dynamic economy is that there will always be uncertainty and lack of information, particularly about the future. My plan is to annually return 2 percent of discretionary spending to the American taxpayers so that *they* can decide how best to utilize their money based on their needs (present and future) rather than the needs of the government. This is what a free-market economy is all about: actualizing decentralized decision-making while giving individuals the means to do so.

My labor force policies will provide practical and effective solutions both short and long term. Not only will my policies help individuals restore their self-worth and revamp their skills, but they will also benefit our communities, reduce inflation, increase economic growth, and help us reach our potential both as individuals and as a nation.

As an added bonus, my policies, by increasing the labor force, will also reduce spending on means-tested programs such as Medicaid, which in turn will help reduce the federal budget deficit (see chapter 6).

CHAPTER 4

Becoming Energy Independent

W atch the construction of any building, and you'll notice the care taken to construct a viable supportive foundation, digging down to the bedrock and establishing adequate supporting posts, without which the building would topple. Indeed, a foundation is critical in all aspects of our lives. We only start a business after laying the careful groundwork, and we begin our college education only after solid preparatory work in high school.

**MY TWO-CENTS PLAN
ON ENERGY**

Promote domestic energy and ensure that USA companies lead the way in promoting clean energy and reducing global warming emissions.

It is illusory to assume that we can construct a building by ignoring its foundation. It is also illusory (and folly) to assume that no matter our long-run energy goals, we can instantly quit our reliance on fossil fuels and click our heels three times to magically awaken to a land of renewable energy. In past energy transitions, (i.e., from water to wood to coal to oil) it took forty to fifty years for an energy source to go from a 1 percent market share to a 10 percent market share. Another century to reach 50 percent, while in the meantime, existing energy sources *continued* to be used.[1] There is no reason to expect this energy transition to be any different, despite quixotic exhortations to the contrary. As Figure 4.1 indicates, not only are we heavily dependent on fossil fuels, but renewables only account for 12.5 percent of our total energy consumption.

Figure 4.1 USA energy consumption by fuel type, 2021

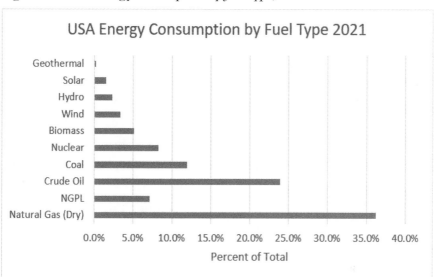

According to Mr. Rhodes's timeline, we still have a long way to go before we reach the magical land of renewable energy. Needless to say, our current energy sources must remain a part of our energy strategy, especially if we do not intend to immediately stop driving, flying, heating our homes, and powering our computers.

Brigham McCown, director of the Hudson Institute's American Energy Security Initiative, agrees and extends Mr. Rhodes' argument:

> Policymakers should ensure the energy mix is comprised of fuel sources that are available, reliable, and affordable while simultaneously guaranteeing the resiliency of our energy and transportation infrastructure. Resiliency means providing the right fuel source to

where and when it is needed without interruption. While the mix of renewables will undoubtedly grow over time, today's high prices directly reflect the absence of sufficient supplies of fossil fuels in our current energy mix. Facilitating higher domestic oil and gas production by curbing excessive permitting and approval processes will address runaway energy costs – especially as we have promised to come to Europe's rescue by providing them with fossil energy supplies this winter. Meaningful change can occur almost overnight by ordering executive branch agencies to act with a sense of urgency as the current dilatory pace is choking the country's efficiency and productivity.[2]

Interestingly, nuclear power only accounts for 8.3 percent of USA energy consumption but 19.6 percent of total USA electricity production (not shown in this table).[3] The reason for the discrepancy is that nuclear energy is used almost entirely to produce electricity, whereas electricity is also produced from coal and natural gas.

As Figure 4.2 indicates, global energy consumption is not that much different, with a slightly higher percentage devoted to fossil fuels (84 percent). This is due to a greater reliance on coal by developing nations, especially India and China. (When these statistics are updated in 2023 expect an increase in fossil fuels across the board, especially coal.)

Despite the Biden administration's wishful thinking, our energy transition is long and arduous, and any net–zero emissions economy requires careful planning. It also requires a firm knowledge of our current energy situation *and* how our current energy sources can help us transition to whatever energy future we want. Only such knowledge can provide us with a good foundation for a vibrant economy.

As a nation we must be honest about what we can and cannot do, for only then can we see the obstacles ahead. It is time to stop fooling ourselves. It is time for our politicians to take a reality energy check and be honest with Americans.

Figure 4.2 Global energy consumption by fuel type, 2020

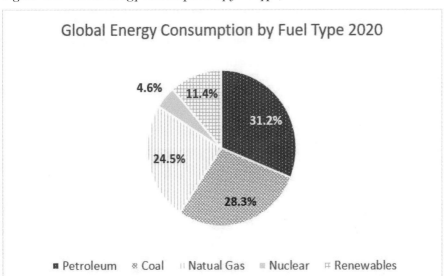

Energy Policies

My energy policies starkly differ from those of the Biden administration. For starters, I recognize our current dependence on fossil fuels, and that in order to transition from our current situation to a net-zero emissions by 2050. If that is our goal (and if it is, it must be reached by democratic consensus and not by executive order), we cannot stop using fossil fuels now, for our current energy sources will (and must) continue to play an important role. In addition, my reality-based policies will help reduce emissions of global warming gases.

Get the oil and natural gas industries on board.

Joe Biden hastily dismissed the oil industry when he became president, disparaging it as "yesterday's fuel," while ignoring the stark reality that fossil fuels are *today's* fuels and will continue to be for quite some time. Understanding this requires the federal government to reassure oil executives, both big and small, that oil is still today's fuel, not just for the USA but for the world. We need short-term action and long-term smarts. Why should we negotiate with Iran, Saudi Arabia, and Venezuela when we should be encouraging and incentivizing our own oil companies, big and small? They have the smarts to enable us to become energy independent.

Cartoon 14 – Biden Assigns Homework

Finish the Keystone Pipeline

Not only is it important to increase energy supplies and reduce prices, but it is important to send a signal that the administration is on the same side of producing more energy for America. Once construction of the Keystone Pipeline is finally underway it will send the oil industry (and the world) a message that we are serious about producing additional supply, which in turn will induce investment optimism and increase other investment projects.

Reduce the Regulations

In its efforts to reach the magical 2050 goal of renewable energy, and in the face of much historical evidence to the contrary, the Biden administration has purposively made it much more difficult to drill for oil and natural gas. It initially suspended new oil and gas leases but now allows only a trickle. It has charged higher federal land drilling fees, and it has pushed the Federal Reserve to implement climate change policies well beyond its congressional mandate of price stability and full employment.

Cartoon 15 – Biden's Creative Energy Tax Team

Needless to say, we need to *immediately* reverse these policies. The federal government must meet with oil and natural gas executives to discuss fruitful policies to increase drilling and domestic supply. By increasing the domestic supply, energy prices will be reduced, which in turn will ease long-run inflation.

The Democrats seem to have forgotten that we are currently heavily dependent on fossil fuels and that energy transition takes time. He has done everything in his power to discourage and to prevent our energy companies from doing their job of providing the American people with reliable energy. This contravenes the energy policies of other US presidents. As Daniel Yergin, vice chairperson of S&P global notes: "Whether Democrats or Republicans, presidents have wanted to embrace the idea of energy independence and production."

A good example of Biden's counterproductive energy strategy is his executive order calling for a moratorium on new oil and gas drilling on federal lands and offshore. Keeping a campaign promise, and catering to the Democratic left, this moratorium was imposed immediately upon taking office. (Federal leases currently account for about 25 percent of US domestic oil and gas production.) Fortunately, there was nothing the Biden administration could do about the legally binding contracts that were signed by previous administrations.

However, as you can see Biden has done everything in his power to minimize the production of oil on federal lands. According to the *Wall Street Journal*, during its first nineteen months, the Biden administration leased only 126,228 federal acres to oil and gas companies. This is the lowest level since Harry Truman when offshore drilling was in its infancy. (This amount is down 97 percent from Trump's first nineteen months.) During his first nineteen months in office, Biden's Interior Department awarded 203 leases for oil and natural gas development. Compare this to the Trump and Obama administrations, who each approved ten times as many.[4] (Biden's 203 leases amount to only 3.2 percent of the leases awarded on average from Eisenhower to Trump!)

Although the number of federal leases has trended downward since President Reagan's record-setting 48 million acres in his first nineteen months (due to increased focus on fracking on private and state- owned lands, and less attention to offshore drilling), Biden's gratuitous moratorium is asinine. Not to mention that it is illegal. In June 2021, a federal judge ruled that the self-imposed moratorium violated the 1920 Mineral

Leasing Act, which requires onshore oil or gas leasing at least quarterly. During Biden's first six quarters in office, only the second quarter of 2022 had any leases, and this was due to higher oil prices resulting from the Russian invasion of Ukraine.[5] Not surprisingly, the Biden administration took this opportunity to charge oil and gas companies a higher royalty. This is yet another example of Biden's policies that will add to inflation. However, *The Wall Street Journal* reports that the Biden administration awarded $190 million of offshore oil-and-gas leases in mid-September as mandated by the IRA. Nevertheless, this leaves Biden "far behind his recent predecessors and put[s] him roughly on par with former presidents Lyndon Johnson and Richard Nixon."[6]

Encourage Innovation

Capitalism has a long history of finding solutions to specific energy problems, ranging from James Watt's development of the steam engine, allowing more coal to be extracted from deeper mines, to George Westinghouse's electrical transformers permitting the long-distance transmission of electricity.[7] The entrepreneurial spirit is best encouraged by reducing the regulatory burden and tax rates, so that entrepreneurs can do what they do best: innovate.

We need intelligent actions now to obtain workable results in the future. The federal government must make it a top priority to unleash the American entrepreneurial spirit, especially in procuring energy by incentivizing our energy producers, while eliminating disincentives.

Rely on US natural gas producers to reduce global methane emissions.

That's right! There is no typo, and I will gladly repeat it: Rely on US natural gas producers to reduce global methane emissions.

A significant problem of natural gas production and distribution is escaped methane (with about 9 percent escaping into the atmosphere) especially during the pipeline transmission to the final user. While CO_2 gets a lot of bad press as the preponderant global warming gas, methane is far more potent and long-lasting in the atmosphere. One ton of escaped methane provides as much greenhouse gases as eighty tons of CO_2.

Innovations by US companies have enabled US natural gas producers to locate methane leaks with pinpoint accuracy, resulting in a significant reduction in methane emissions. Compare this to Russia, one of the world's most environmentally inefficient natural gas producers. Russian natural gas exported to Germany (Europe's largest importer of Russian natural gas) is twice as damaging to the environment due to leaking methane emissions as the same amount of natural gas imported from the USA.[8]

We are all part of the same world. The overall effect on our environment of our energy policies is a cumulative tally of our actions. So, unless we intend to immediately stop driving, flying, and heating our homes, it is in the world's best interest to have the USA produce as much oil and natural gas as possible.

I should point out that 17 percent of USA natural gas production is ESG (Environmental, Social, and Governance) certified. Yes, I said that right! I know ESG standards have received a fair share of criticism. *The Economist* magazine, for example, called them "exaggerated, superficial, guff." The criticisms are well taken, suggesting that perhaps we need to develop a more sophisticated measure. But right now, despite its flaws, ESG is all we have. Having said that, this is an amazing, eye-opening statistic, one that surely makes environmentalists cringe. How can a fossil fuel company be ESG certified? But, at the same time, this statistic underscores my point: since we are not in a position to immediately switch to renewable energy, encouraging and developing our fossil fuels so that they actively reduce global warming is not only the best road taken, but at least for the foreseeable future, the only road available.[9]

Make liquefied natural gas (LNG) a global priority.

Natural gas cannot be transported across the oceans via pipelines. It must first be supercooled to a liquid and then turned back into a gas at the receiving port. This requires sophisticated conversion ports at both ends, which not all countries possess. Germany, for example, Europe's largest economy and its largest importer of Russian natural gas, possesses no liquefied natural gas (LNG) ports (either sending or receiving). The USA is currently the world's largest producer of LNG, but to really make LNG work, we need a global commitment led by USA technology. But alas, such ports are not built overnight. The federal government working with our energy companies should make this a top priority. Switching to LNG not only will reduce methane emissions, but it will also lessen the reliance on Russian natural gas.

Resuscitate our moribund nuclear industry.

It is hard to believe that the US, which pioneered peaceful nuclear energy (converting uranium into electricity) currently has only one operating uranium mill. Why is this, when the USA has more nuclear reactors with 92, than any other country in the world?[10]

Of interest and of concern are the numbers for nuclear reactors under construction, nuclear reactors planned (expected to be operating within the next fifteen years), and proposed reactors. The numbers are startling and raise concern about the viability and price stability of uranium, perhaps pointing to the need to develop fusion and other fusion materials. The numbers also raise concerns about China's preponderant role in uranium.[11] This data is not a license to panic, only an invitation to plan ahead, and to actively develop the technology that will allow us to develop alternative sources of both fissionable and fusionable materials. Now is the time to plan before it is too late to act.

Figure 4.3 World Nuclear reactors as of 2022

Reactors Under Construction: 60 Globally	
China	22 (36.7% of total)
India	8 (13.3% of total)

Reactors Planned: 96 Globally	
China	38 (39.6% of total)
Russia	25 (26.0% of total)
India	12 (12.5% of total)

Reactors Proposed: 332 Globally	
China	160 (48.2% of total)
India	28 (8.4% of total)
Russia	21 (6.3% of total)

Source: World Nuclear Association, September 2022

USA uranium mining peaked at 43.7 million tons in the late 1970s and has since dwindled to 10.5 tons, largely due to cheaper uranium imports from Canada and Australia.[12] Today, 14 percent of our uranium imports come from Russia. (Why are we importing anything from Russia?) Unfortunately, Russia is currently the only global supplier of a specific uranium needed for newly designed reactors, but hopefully we can soon change that. The USA imports 43 percent of its uranium from the former Soviet republics of Kazakhstan and Uzbekistan, largely still in Russia's orbit.

The federal government should incentivize the Uranium Producers of America, so they can produce *more* uranium cheaply. Since uranium is used to produce electricity, this will reduce energy costs and our dependence on other nations.

The actual production of uranium into electricity produces no global warming gases (although the drilling, processing, and distribution does, by using fossil fuels). Nuclear energy is by far the safest of the non-renewable fuels.[13] Coal, at one extreme has 24.6 deaths per terawatt hour of electricity (largely due to its incidence in the atmosphere), while at the other extreme, nuclear energy is right there with renewables at only 0.03 deaths per terawatt hour. While no energy source can ever be risk-free, nuclear energy clearly offers a palatable and necessary alternative.

Continue to develop a Strategic Uranium Reserve.

This is similar to the Strategic Petroleum Reserve which has a capacity for storing 713.5 million barrels—about a month's worth of oil at current rates of consumption. Established in 1975 after the 1973-1974 oil embargo, the oil is stored in salt caverns in Louisiana and Texas for emergency use to help temper price increases. There is no reason not to do the same with uranium.

Develop a workable and environmentally sustainable policy toward lithium.

Go back 120 years or so, to the infancy of the automobile industry, circa 1900. Of the 4,192 cars produced in the USA, 1,681 were steamers, 1,575 were electrics, and only 936 were internal combustion.[14] Electric cars were popular back then, especially for intra-city driving. But fourteen years later, the internal combustion automobile had won the popularity contest, and never looked back, until at least now. It won because of the supporting infrastructure and the lack thereof for the electric vehicles, especially in inter-city travel.[15]

Today, electric vehicles (EVs) are in a similar position. Their popularity is gaining, save for the lack of infrastructure. But unlike 100 years ago, the development of infrastructure is moving forward. Meanwhile, the demand for EVs is accelerating. There were 2.2. million units sold in 2019 for a 2.5 percent market share, representing a 400 percent increase from 2015; with 11 million units expected to be sold by 2025, and 11-19 million units by 2030. Although as the magazine cautions, this could be a significant underestimate.[16]

While EVs do not emit tailpipe emissions—hence their attractiveness; their full life cycle tells a different story. The mining production and refinement of lithium, a key ingredient in the construction of EV batteries, requires extensive use of fossil fuels. So how and where lithium is made into batteries matters for the environment.

According to *Investing News* reporter Melissa Pistilli,

> While lithium production in China is comparatively low, it is the largest consumer of lithium due to its electronics manufacturing and EV industries. It also produces more than three-quarters of the world's lithium-ion batteries, and controls most of the world's lithium-processing facilities.[17]

Electric cars require batteries. Unfortunately, 79 percent of the world's lithium batteries are produced in China which uses coal as its primary energy source. This has an enormously negative impact on the environment. It is ironic given that the main motivation of buyers of EVs is to help the environment, its locus of production is making matters worse. According to *Industry Week*, "Just to build each car battery—weighing upwards of 500 kilograms (1,100 pounds) in size for sport-utility vehicles—would emit up to 74 percent more CO_2 than producing an efficient conventional car if it's made in a factory powered by fossil fuels."[18]

To help the global environment and to make the world a better place, we need to shift the production of lithium batteries to the USA. Doing so would reduce the production of global gases given the tendency of the USA to use natural gas rather than coal.[19]

Currently the USA only produces about 1 percent of total lithium production[20] while possessing 3.4 percent of global lithium reserves,[21] although this could change soon as there seems to be some uncertainty of the total amount of global reserves and the effectiveness of bringing such reserves to market based on technology and market price. There is no reason why the USA should not be a major player in the industry, shifting the focus away from China.

Incentivize Ethanol Producers

Ethanol is a grain alcohol that is blended with gasoline and helps reduce carbon emissions. The USA is the world's largest ethanol producer, producing twice as much as the second largest producer, Brazil. Here in the USA, Iowa is our largest producer, accounting for about a third of total US production.[22] Using ethanol is a sensible way of ensuring adequate energy supplies.

The Geopolitics of Fossil Fuels

Figures 4.5, 4.6, and 4.7 depict the world's largest producers of oil, natural, gas, and coal, respectively. Notice that the USA is the world's largest natural gas producer, followed by Russia; with Iran, China, and Qatar, a distant third, fourth and fifth, respectively (with their combined output just about half that of the USA). The USA is the world's largest producer of oil, currently producing 14.5 percent of global supply. The USA is also the world's largest importer of oil. Although Russia is not in the top five for coal producers, it ranks seventh just behind Australia.

Figure 4.4 The world's top five oil producers, 2021

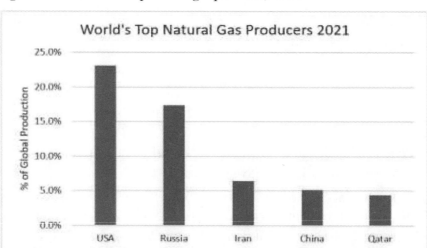

Source: https://www.visualcapitalist.com/visualizing-the-worlds-largest-oil-producers/#:~:text=The%20Largest%20Oil%20Producers%20in,%2C%20Saudi%20Arabia%2C%2 0and%20Russia.

Figure 4.5 The world's top natural gas producers, 2021

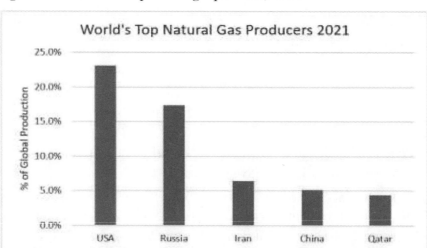

Source: https://worldpopulationreview.com/country-rankings/natural-gas-by-country

Figure 4.6 The world's top coal producers, 2021

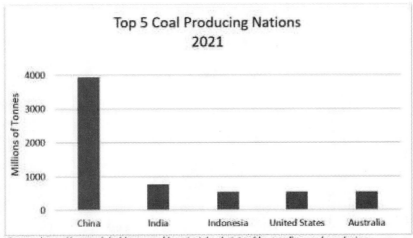

Source: https://www.globaldata.com/data-insights/mining/the-top-five-coal-producing-countries-million-tonnes-2021/

But just as important (if not more so) is who controls the fossil fuel reserves. Figures 4.7, 4.8, and 4.9, depict the largest reserve owners of oil, natural gas, and coal, respectively.

Figure 4.7 The world's top owners of oil reserves[23]

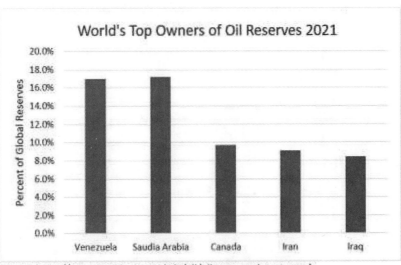

Source: https://www.worldometers.info/oil/oil-reserves-by-country/

Figure 4.8 The world's top owners of natural gas reserves, 2021

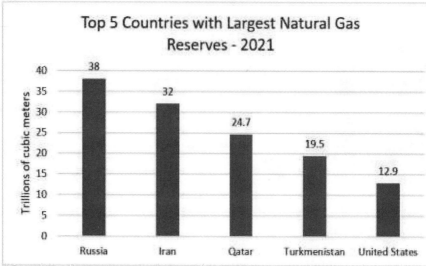

Source: https://www.nsenergybusiness.com/features/biggest-natural-gas-reserves-countries/

Figure 4.9 The world's top owners of coal reserves, 2021

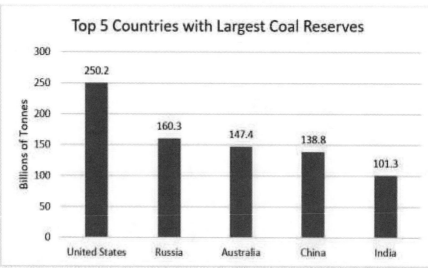

Source: https://www.mining-technology.com/analysis/feature-the-worlds-biggest-coal-reserves-by-country/

While neither Russia nor the USA is in the top five for oil reserves, Russia is the world's largest owner of natural gas reserves (the USA is the third) and the second largest owner of coal reserves, after the USA.

Oil and natural gas have always been used as political weapons. Currently Russia, as the world's second largest gas producer and the largest owner of gas reserves, is using its clout and leverage to influence its neighbors (especially the heavily dependent Germany and the Baltic states) by either cutting off or reducing supply. As existing energy contracts end and new ones are consummated, prices will significantly increase causing significant pain. This is not expected to end after only one winter.

Since 2011, revenue from crude oil and natural gas has comprised 43 percent of Russian government revenue. After Russia's invasion of Ukraine, western nations have imposed sanctions on crude oil and natural gas. But these have been ineffectual, instead making Russia richer rather than poorer, despite reducing its level of exports. In May 2022, Russia earned €883 million per day from oil exports, up from €633 million in May 2021.[24] So, the aggressor benefits while global oil customers suffer. The aggressor can funnel its oil and natural gas revenue to its war machine. Where is the justice in that?

My energy policies will increase our domestic supply of oil and natural gas by unburdening our domestic producers from Biden's regulations and supply-side restrictions. This in turn will not only ease long-run inflation but, as we discussed earlier, reduce global warming gases. Just as importantly, it will reduce funding for Russia's war machine. My policies will help ease Europe's suffering by increasing US's supply, which in turn will reduce global gas prices and global warming emissions.

The Economist advocates increasing alternative sources of supply,[25] which is exactly what the Biden administration has refused to do and exactly what my policy is all about. Not only are my energy policies best for the USA and the free world, they are the only ones that make sense *at this point in time.* We need short-term action and long-term thinking. My Two-Cents plan will deliver.

To punish Russia, the Biden administration has called for a buyer's cartel in which the major consumers of Russian oil act as one concerted buyer, with an artificially established price much lower than the current market price, yet high enough to allow Russia to make a profit. This scheme will supposedly benefit oil consumers while reducing the revenue funneled to Russia's military.[26]

Cartoon 16 – Person of the Year—Whose Year?

Cartels like the well-known Organization of Petroleum Exporting Countries (which by the way is a producer's cartel), however, are notoriously difficult to control. Keep in mind they have all the power because they have something we need. But if our objective is to reduce Russia's oil and gas revenue to reduce the money funneled into their war machine, then isn't it best to tackle the problem at its source? Unleash the forces of supply and demand to free limitations on drilling and mining, thereby increasing supply of oil and gas, reducing their price, and reducing global warming gases.

Relying on market forces to lower prices is a well-established solution; relying on a contrived cartel is not. Let us put ourselves in a position of strength and effectuate policies with a proven track record.

Conclusion

Our oil and natural gas industries are currently the world's most environmentally friendly. We should lead the way forward to help other nations (especially developing nations that heavily rely on coal and are in no position to switch to renewable energy) achieve energy independence, while at the same time decreasing carbon emissions. Let's unleash the power of US technology to make this happen.

If the US wants to be really energy independent, we need short-term action and long-term thinking:

Short-term actions: recognize our dependence on oil and natural gas. Let's have policies that will eliminate suffocating regulations and artificial supply-side restrictions on oil and natural gas production and increase domestic uranium production.

Long-term thinking: It is important to realize that we are always going to have energy needs. Therefore, it is important that we are actively thinking about developing new energy sources and new ways of producing existing energy. As time goes on, we will probably have discoveries that will enable us to be increasingly favorable and friendly to our environment. I have always been a proponent of Americans being at the forefront of innovation.

CHAPTER 5

Fixing the Border

R ecords, records, records! But not the kind that merits boasting.

The mess on our southern border with Mexico is appalling and deeply troubling to all Americans. So much so that I do not know where to begin. Picking out any problem to start with implicitly assumes that the others are less important. But all are important, and they cumulatively present an atrocious situation which absolutely cannot continue. It makes a mockery of our law and order. Where is the law on our borders? Where is the order?

**MY TWO-CENTS PLAN
ON IMMIGRATION:**

Secure our international borders by ending all illegal immigration, while encouraging legal immigration.

The blame starts and ends with Biden. Although, it is not exactly blaming since the record speaks for itself. Perhaps more accurately: our border mess is due to Biden's policies. Or lack thereof. Let us with some statistics:

- In 2021, the Border Patrol reported a record 1,659,206 encounters with migrants[1] illegally trying to enter the USA (see Figure 5.1).[2]

- This record bested the previous highs of 1,643,679 in 2000 and 1,615,844 in 1986.[3] The data for 2022 is not all in yet, but it has already exceeded 2.2 million, indicating that the 2021 record will easily be broken.

Figure 5.1 USA Border Encounters

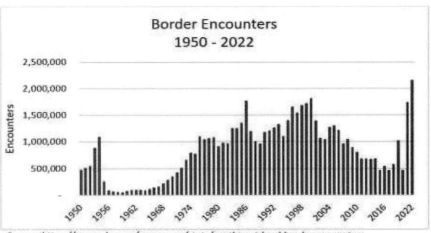

Source: https://www.cbp.gov/newsroom/stats/southwest-land-border-encounters
https://www.dhs.gov/immigration-statistics/yearbook/2019/table33

- In 2021, Mexico was the number one origin country for illegal migrants with 608,037 encounters, accounting for 37 percent. The remaining 1,051,169 encounters, or 63 percent of the illegal migrants, involved people from countries other than Mexico— the highest total on record.

- In 2019, only 9 percent of USA Border Patrol apprehensions involved nations beyond Mexico and the Northern Triangle (El Salvador, Guatemala, Honduras).[4] But in 2022, 40 percent of the illegal border encounters involved nations beyond these four—a record! Incidentally, the record was 22 percent in 2021.[5] Way to go Joe!

- In only one year (from 2020 to 2021) the USA witnessed a staggering increase in illegal immigrants from countries not usually connected to US immigration (see Figures 4.2 and 4.3): Haiti from 4,395 in 2020 to 45,532 in 2021; Cuba (9,822 to 38,139); Venezuela (1,227 to 47,752); Brazil (6,946 to 56,735); Romania (266 to 2,029); and Turkey (67 to 1,366).[6]

This is sort of like trick or treating on Halloween, with cars and sometimes even buses trekking kids from one neighborhood to another in search of better candy, overwhelming the neighborhood's resources. But unlike the innocence of trick or treating, such illegal immigration makes a mockery of the sanctity of national borders. It makes a mockery of our claim to be a nation of law and order.

Figure 5.2 2019 Border Encounters: Country of Origin

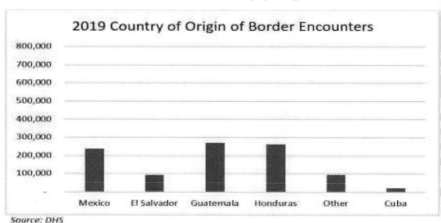

Source: DHS

Figure 5.3 2022 Border Encounters: Country of Origin

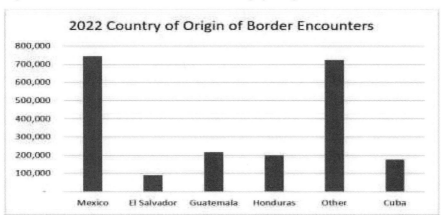

Source: DHS

- The rate of recidivism (i.e., illegal immigrants caught and denied entry once, then trying again) has significantly increased since 2020, reaching a record 27 percent in 2021. This is partly due to Title 42, first implemented in 1944 as part of the Public Health Services Act to prevent the spread of communicable diseases. The Trump administration invoked Title 42 in March 2020 to protect against COVID, enabling the Border Patrol to turn away anyone for health-related reasons.[7] Given the circumstances, which was a reasonable response. The problem, however, is that under this act, illegal immigrants are merely turned away, incentivizing most, if not all, to try again; whereas before March 2020, anyone caught was criminally prosecuted and detained possibly for months. From the immigrant's perspective, why not try again? What is there to lose? Rather than incentivizing illegal aliens to attempt to cross our borders, we need to incentivize them not to do so.

While we know the actual number of illegal border encounters, we do not know the number of "gotaways" (i.e., immigrants who enter illegally and undetected. Ieva Jusionyte, an associate professor on international security at Brown University, told *Newsweek* that "At the end of the day, we just don't know what we don't know—that is, how many people succeed in crossing the border without being apprehended." While President Biden touts the increased number of encounters as evidence that his immigration policies are working, and Vice President Kamala Harris boasts that the southern border is secure, both are wrong and neither knows for sure. How can they? Who are they trying to fool? It could just as well be interpreted that the high number of illegal border encounters represents more people entering the USA illegally. It is a sad state of affairs that not only is the number of gotaways not known but that we are allowing this to happen in the first place.[8]

The Federation for American Immigration Reform (FAIR) estimates that approximately 900,000 gotaways have entered the USA illegally since Biden took office. Although given that we just don't know what we don't know, this can only be an estimate, and a conservative one at that. In August 2022, Dan Stein, president of FAIR wrote that roughly the

> equivalent of the entire population of Ireland has illegally entered the United States in the 18 months since President Biden has been in office, with many being released into American communities. In that time, the Biden administration has blamed an unprecedented surge of illegal immigration on all sorts of external factors, except their own sabotage of our nation's immigration laws. The endless flow of illegal aliens and the incursion of lethal narcotics pouring across our border will not end until this administration demonstrates a willingness to enforce our laws.[9]

I absolutely agree. We need law and order everywhere in the USA, and especially on our borders. How many of these illegal immigrants are criminals? How many are terrorists? How do these people interact with the local communities? Sadly, since we do not know the number of gotaways, we cannot answer these questions. Since we cannot answer these questions, we do not know how much our national security has deteriorated since Joe Biden was elected president. A sad state of affairs.

Since President Biden assumed office in 2021, approximately 1.3 million illegal immigrants, many of whom are seeking asylum, have been temporarily allowed into the USA, according to the FAIR. These are not gotaways since we know who these people are. Add this to the gotaways, and the Biden administration has let in approximately 2.3 million illegal migrants since taking office. Unbelievable. FAIR conservatively estimates that each illegal migrant costs each USA taxpayer $9,232 per year. Step back a minute and imagine spending this money on programs that Americans actually need, which could easily

- fund the hiring of 330,000 new teachers (going a long way to end America's longstanding teacher shortage)

- provide every homeless veteran in America $50,000 per year for a decade and end veteran homelessness

- give every family in America earning $50k or less a grocery voucher of roughly $410

- provide Supplemental Nutrition Assistance Program (SNAP) benefits to more than 7 million additional needy families

- fund and expand the entire National School Lunch Program; hire more than 315,000 police officers to combat rising crime across the country

- pay for the construction of nearly the entire Southern Border Wall[10]

Dan Stein illustrates the misguided values of Biden's so-called immigration policies, or lack thereof:

Even in an age in which trillion-dollar spending packages are considered modest, the additional $20.4 billion the Biden Border Crisis has

heaped onto the backs of American taxpayers is still staggering…
$20.4 billion could address some very important needs of the American public, instead of covering the costs of the surge of illegal migration triggered by this administration's policies […] 35 percent of U.S. families with a full-time worker struggle to meet their basic needs. These are the people President Biden pledged to champion. Instead, he is choosing to divert an additional $20.4 billion away from their needs, in order to fund a radical open borders agenda with no end in sight.[11]

- The $20.4 billion, as troubling as it is, does not include the $140 billion annual cost to USA taxpayers to provide benefits and services for the *existing* illegal aliens, of which there are estimated to be approximately 11 million. Yikes!

- In a really disturbing report by FAIR, as if these other reports have not been disturbing—ha! the effects of illegal immigration have adversely affected our public-school systems. Once again Dan Stein weighs in:

As a nation, we are failing to adequately educate the next generation of workers and taxpayers – even those for whom English is their native tongue. At the same time, our immigration policies are adding millions of LEP [Limited English Proficient] students, whose academic prospects are even more abysmal. Under the Biden administration, our failing educational system is being asked to cope with our failed immigration policies, which is a recipe for disaster.[12]

In the first six months of 2022, there were 609 (illegal) migrant deaths compared to 566 in all of 2021 (see Figure 5.4). Another record!

Figure 5.4 Migrant Deaths

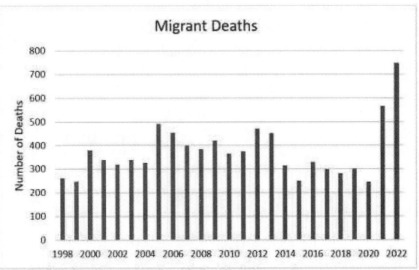

Note: Number of Deaths = number of remains found by border patrol.
Source: https://borderoversight.org/2022/09/08/7805-migrant-remains-found-by-
border-patrol-in-22-years/

Perhaps before we move on you should take an Alka-Seltzer to calm your stomach or step out for some fresh air since we are not done yet.

Let's take a further look at Biden's immigration policies, or more accurately the lack thereof:

- President Biden has also made use of the Deferred Enforced De-parture, which under the president's discretion, offers protection from catastrophes in the immigrant's home country.

- In August 2022, the Biden administration lifted the Trump's 2019 "Remain in Mexico rule, which required that all migrants seeking asylum to remain in Mexico until their US immigration court date.

- On the first day of his administration, President Biden dramati-cally reversed former president Donald Trump's border policies, which had gone a long way to stemming the tide of illegal im-migrants. This has, not surprisingly, incentivized the number of migrants seeking to enter the USA.

Before we look at my immigration policies for both illegal and legal immigration, you might need a breath of fresh air. Take your time. Then, when you return, we briefly discuss the nature, causes, and effects of legal immigration (and emigration). This is necessary in order to understand how my immigration policies will incentivize legal immigration, while disincentivizing illegal immigration.

The Nature, Causes, and Effects of Legal Immigration

One of the most gut-wrenching decisions an individual has to make during his or her life is to leave his or her native country. Think of it: bidding farewell to your culture, food, language, friends, and family and going somewhere foreign, somewhere new. Perhaps because it is so emotional and so difficult, it should not be surprising that individuals who have left their native country (i.e., emigrated) comprise only 3.5 percent of the global population, that is, 272 million migrants.

Even though this number is low (or at least perceived to be), it has been recently increasing and is expected to accelerate. (see Figure 5.5).

Figure 5.5 Global Migration, as a percent of total population, 1950-2021

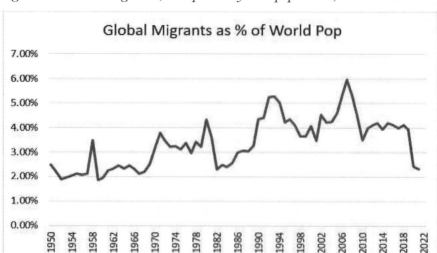

https://population.un.org/wpp/Download/Standard/MostUsed/

Of course, one does not leave one's native land for trivial reasons, because you don't like the look of a tree across the street. Through the millennia, the reasons for emigration have remained fairly constant:

- famine
- war
- religious and political persecution
- drought
- lack of opportunity
- revolution
- drugs and violence

For the USA all these factors have at various times played a key role in both the number and composition of immigrants coming to our shores. Perhaps not surprisingly the USA leads the world in the absolute number of immigrants (absolute in terms of numbers rather than as a percent of the home population) as Figure 5.6 indicates:

Figure 5.6 Top five nations with the highest number of immigrants

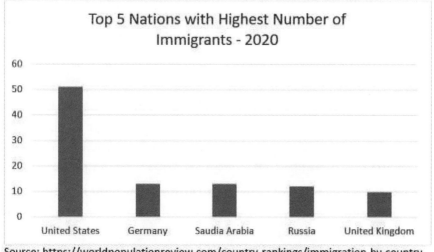

Source: https://worldpopulationreview.com/country-rankings/immigration-by-country

Surprisingly, the next three nations following the USA are Germany, Saudi Arabia, and Russia. Each has actively welcomed migrants from its immediate orbit and/or sphere of influence. Rounding out the top five is the United Kingdom, which has long been known for its open-door policy.

Every nation claims its jurisdictional right to determine the sanctity of its borders pertaining to who can be let in and who can be let out. Although it is incumbent on our federal government to actively ensure our borders are as secure as possible, that does not mean we completely prohibit *legal* immigrants. Border security and immigration are two different matters. As we discussed in the previous section, the Biden administration has failed miserably in stopping illegal immigrants; instead it is actually incentivizing them. My immigration policies will redress this miserable failure, but first we must take a more in-depth look at *legal* immigration.

Our great nation has three options pertaining to *legal* immigration: (1) close our borders and not allow any legal entry; (2) let every legal immigrant in, while at the same time expanding the definition of legal immigrants since only legal immigrants can enter; or (3) ration the number of legal immigrants.

The first option not only goes against our great tradition of welcoming "your tired, your poor, your huddled masses yearning to breathe free," (Emma Lazarus, 1883) but it is a recipe for economic stagnation. Take Japan, for example. Priding itself on cultural homogeneity, it severely restricts the number of immigrants. Combine this with Japan's lowest birth rate on record, and they have a shrinking population and the world's oldest nation. Japan's rate of population growth, after peaking in 1972, has steadily declined and has actually been negative for the last six years. Twenty-five percent of Japan's population is sixty-five or older. By comparison, here in the USA, only 17 percent of our population is older than sixty-five.

A greying Japanese population together with tight restrictions on immigration has meant (and will continue to mean) a shrinking population and a shrinking economy, loss of global status, and a much greater burden on working people to support the nonworking elderly. In this sense Japan provides us with a model of what *not* to do, especially given that our birth rate has also been declining, like it has for all western nations. But unlike Japan, we have historically welcomed immigrants to our shores, although as Figure 5.7 illustrates the numbers have significantly varied over the years.

Figure 5.7 USA Net Immigration 1950 - 2021 (Legal)

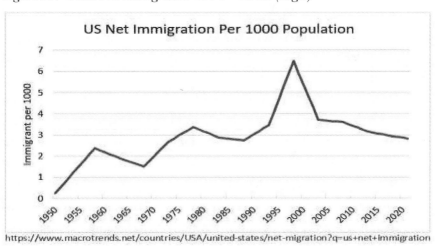

https://www.macrotrends.net/countries/USA/united-states/net-migration?q=us+net+immigration

Very troubling, however, is that our net number of immigrants (accounting for both entering and leaving, authorized and unauthorized) is currently at historical lows. From July 2020 to July 2021, it was plus 247,000, the smallest in thirty years and about one-third of the annual average during that period. COVID was partly to blame as America (like most nations) limited visitors, closed consulates, and froze applications; but the decline in immigration predates COVID. In 2017, for example, the Trump administration implemented high-profile restrictions on Muslim immigrants and made the entire immigration process lengthier, more tedious, and more costly, increasing the frustration of all concerned.

During the 2010s, new immigrants accounted for 70 percent of the growth in the American labor force. If the pre-2010 trend in immigration had continued, the labor force would increase to 178 million by 2040, instead of continuing to decrease. Given that immigrants during the next two decades are likely to be the only source of labor force growth (unless my labor force policies discussed in chapter 3 are enacted), the sharp decline in legal immigrants is troubling and will show up in unfilled job openings in all industries relying on foreign labor ranging from restaurants to hotels to gardening to construction. We could have a shortage across all skill levels from day laborers to doctors, engineers, and architects. We may be the only nation that actively discourages legal immigration while simultaneously incentivizing illegal immigration.

America has a roller-coaster history of legal immigration ranging from letting everyone in to restricting immigration by nation, skills, and even one's hemisphere of origin, with wide swings in policy depending on the national mood. Both sides of the aisle have long criticized our immigration policy as a hodgepodge of rules, biases, and ideologies—and rightfully so. Systematic efforts have been made at immigration reform dating to the Bush administration, and every administration has made reform a top priority, with little success.

The 2022 Los Angeles Declaration on Migration provides a hopeful start in the right direction, although key nations for both legal and illegal immigration were absent: Mexico, Cuba, Venezuela, and Nicaragua. Signed in July 2022 in Los Angeles, twenty-one nations pledged to expand *legal* migration and revamp the asylum process, while creating a common denominator across sending or receiving nations. The latter is important since legal immigration (migrants entering) benefits the receiving nation while emigration (migrants leaving) depletes the home labor force and especially skilled workers. This creates a very problematic and self-perpetuating brain drain.

Cartoon 17 – Shortage? Just Skip the Paperwork

Immigration Policies

Any immigration policy must simultaneously focus on three points:

1. Tight and non-porous border security. This is nonnegotiable and a legitimate concern for every nation. Without this there is anarchy.

2. Strict policies to cease and desist illegal immigration. Under no circumstances should illegal immigration be tolerated or encouraged. To do so actively encourages would-be migrants. We need to incentivize people not to become illegal entrants.

3. A policy to welcome *legal* immigrants based on the economic, social, and cultural needs of the host nation. Whether or not it rations the number of legal immigrants should be decided based on its needs rather than the number of applicants.

My specific immigration policies are firmly grounded on this sensible "three-legged stool." They are:

Eliminate the incentive to illegally enter the USA.

We must start by being aware that the United States is truly the land of opportunity. If you lived in a country where you had trouble feeding your family, you would want to live here too. It is important to recognize that the people entering illegally are doing so because they want a better life for themselves and their families. While I have complete sympathy for their goals, I also know that every country, including ours, has a right to its own sovereignty. This is a reason why no nation allows people to enter illegally. In fact, when I go overseas, I am required to have a passport and in some countries a visa. I suggest we secure the border and restore normalcy by making it less porous.

Increase the number of legal immigrants.

We must do our best to encourage legal immigrants (see below) while keeping out those with criminal records, potential terrorists, and anyone else deemed unfit by national security. Allowing more legal immigrants to enter the USA is a win-win situation for all: workers will be hired into the job openings, more goods and services will be produced, supply chains will be strengthened, inflation will decrease, productivity will increase, and increased local spending will boost business optimism and energize the entrepreneurial spirit.

But what about legal immigrants taking our jobs? Research has shown that legal immigrants do not take away existing jobs except perhaps at the very bottom of the skill level, although these jobs are not being filled by our own workers.[13] Legal immigrants contribute to the local dynamism of their communities and help boost overall spending, business optimism, and aggregate demand. If the number of legal immigrants allowed to enter the USA is tailored to specific local needs of our communities, then our economy benefits. Most legal immigrants want to work and want to contribute to a better America for themselves and their children. Isn't this what the American Dream is all about?

The federal government must work directly with business groups and the Chamber of Commerce to facilitate and encourage increased legal immigration: Every business group, the chambers of commerce, and the Big Tech firms have been actively lobbying the federal government for additional legal immigrants to fill the USA's 10.1 million job openings. Currently, for example, the restaurant and accommodations industries, which fill one-fourth of its employees from immigrants, are not able to fill 15 percent of their openings. Professional and business services, where the foreign-born account for 20 percent of their employees, cannot fill 10 percent of its openings.[14]

The business firm is a central feature of our capitalist economy, and the federal government should give every firm the necessary tools for them to do their jobs so that they can produce the necessary goods and services that Americans need while making a profit. Increased legal immigration is what American businesses want, and the federal government must do everything reasonably possible to ensure that their demands are met. There is no reason why we should wait until migrants arrive in the USA to connect them with employers. We have the technology to at least begin the process in the immigrants' home nations.

Streamline the laborious entry process for legal immigrants.

Fixing the entry process for legal immigrants requires immediate attention. Currently, 410,000 people are waiting for State Department interviews to obtain a green card, with only thirty thousand interviews scheduled per month.[15]

Work with Mexico on immigration and emigration solutions.

Given that we share a two-thousand-mile border with Mexico, it should not be surprising that Mexico is our largest source of immigrants, both documented and undocumented. In addition, Mexico is the largest conduit for illegal immigrants from Latin America and the rest of the world (see the above discussion). Thanks to Biden's porous border policies, the record number of non-Mexican immigrants streaming across the border recently has been eye-opening.

A Note on Cuban Immigrants

Given Cuba's geographical proximity to the USA (only ninety miles away) and the sharp difference in living standards between the two nations, it should be no surprise that from the early nineteenth century onwards a steady stream of Cuban immigrants—including professionals, merchants, landowners, cigar makers, political refugees, and an assortment of others—has entered the USA and settled in New York City, Philadelphia, New Orleans, Key West, and Tampa.

Since the 1959 overthrow of the Cuban government by socialist Fidel Castro, immigration (and emigration) has taken a more defined political tone. In 1961 America broke diplomatic relations with Cuba, treating Cuban migrants as refugees from communism and offering a fast track to legal and permanent residency. Since the passage of the 1966 Cuban Adjustment Act, Cubans can qualify for permanent USA residency two years after entry. (In 1976, this was shortened to one year). Cubans, by the way, are the only immigrant group with this status. In addition, Cubans are exempt from any immigration quotas or showing a family-based or employment-based reason for residency.

The Cuban government has used emigration to the USA as a political and economic safety valve, releasing surplus labor, political dissidents, and even common criminals and other undesirables, such as occurred during the Mariel Exodus (1980) and the Balsero Crisis (1994).

The Trump administration made Cuban immigration into the USA as difficult as possible, reversing the Obama administration's more lenient policies, by shutting down the Cuban embassy, suspending visa processing, halting all consular services, cutting back on USA family remittances and travel to Cuba, and designating Cuba as a sponsor of terrorism.

Cuba was devasted by COVID. In 2021, its economy shrank by 11 percent and inflation hit 71 percent. Given the constricted legal methods of entry, and the devastating conditions brought about by COVID (not that conditions were that much better before) the number of Cubans trying to enter America illegally sharply increased. Since October 2021, more than 78,000 Cubans have been apprehended at the USA border, the highest number since 1980. The US Coast Guard has prevented nearly 13,000 Cubans and Haitians from reaching the United States in 2022, more than five times the number of migrants intercepted in 2021).[16] Obviously "the continued migration flows of Cubans, both to the US and Mexico, highlight the need for effective pathways for *legal* immigration."[17] There should be no reason why Cubans who want to enter the USA legally should be denied entry. But increasing the legal channels for immigration does not mean that we allow everyone to enter. As a nation, we reserve that right.

Currently, approximately 2.7 million Cubans who were either born in Cuba (1.3 million) or are of family descent, live in the USA; a significant increase from 1.2 million in 2000. Most Cuban Americans live in Florida (66 percent), California (5 percent), and New Jersey (4 percent). I think Cuba is a very important resource for us particularly those who can contribute to our economic growth and well-being.[18]

Conclusion

From a national security and law-and-order perspective, it is urgent that we cease and desist all illegal immigration. There should be no disagreement and no hesitation. From an economic perspective, it is incumbent that we increase legal immigration to help alleviate shortages in skilled labor and to increase our labor force. My immigration policies will restore the sanctity of our borders while also boosting our economy.

CHAPTER 6

Rescuing Social Security and Medicare

I wish I had a dollar for every time a person has asked me: "Is Social Security really going bankrupt? Will I really lose everything I have contributed?" All Americans are concerned, not just the sixty-something-year-olds who are eyeing retirement. A young college student recently said to me, "I don't understand why I have to contribute to Social Security when the stupid thing is going to go bankrupt."

**MY TWO-CENTS PLAN
ON SOCIAL SECURITY AND MEDICARE**

Stabilize Social Security and Medicare by incentivizing work, immigration, and recognizing increased longevity.

Well, two comments: (1) even in the worst-case scenario Social Security will not go bankrupt; there will be funds available, although not everyone's demands will be fully met; and (2) if my plan is instituted, the worst-case scenario will never happen; it will ensure that the Social Security system will continuously be in surplus.

Even though my plan will not directly affect Social Security, its indirect benefits will be a significant positive influence, putting Americans' fears at ease.

Our Social Security System

Think of the Social Security system (also known as Old Age, Survivors, and Disability Insurance, OASDI) as a giant reservoir with water going in and coming out. Tax contributions from wage earners flow in; and money flows out for the retired and/or disabled.

While the OASDI is currently in surplus (more money coming in than going out), the surplus is expected to be depleted in the year 2035. Notice that I did not say that the system itself will be depleted or that the system will run out of funds. This distinction is obviously critical and bears repeating: The current surplus will be depleted, not the Social Security system itself. In 2035 more money will be going out to OASDI beneficiaries than money coming in. Just as the water level drops in a reservoir with more outgoing than incoming water, the same will happen to the Social Security system.

The reason for the projected OASDI deficit in 2035 is simple: we are living longer. The fastest growing demographic group in the USA is people ninety years of age and older. In 1980, this group only comprised 2.8 percent of our population; today that percentage is 4.7 percent, and by 2050, the percentage is projected to reach 10 percent. In 2050, one out of every ten Americans will be ninety or older! According to the Peter G. Peterson Foundation, in 2010 the USA population over 65 was 40.5 million, and after increasing to 56.1 million today, it is expected to increase to 94.7 million in 2060. That's an increase of over 100 percent in just 50 years![1]

Born in 1898, my grandfather died three months shy of his one hundredth birthday. Back then the probability of living to a hundred was 1 in 10,000. Today, one out of three children born this year will live to be one hundred. My great-great-grandmother lived to be 106, beating the 1 in 100,000 odds of reaching one hundred.

So, I have some good news and some *really* good news. The *really* good news: thanks to good family genes, I expect to be around a long time. The good news: I have ceaseless and unbounded energy, fueled by a lifetime of entrepreneurial success, to write this book and to actively work with my fellow Americans to get our great nation back on track.

Today, once Americans reach the age of sixty-five (granted, not an insignificant achievement) our life expectancy has been steadily increasing, except very recently due to the worrisome COVID, although this situation is expected to reverse soon. In 1940, the average remaining life expectancy, *once a person reaches the age of 65,* was 12.7 years for men and 14.7 years for women. Today those numbers are 19.1 and 25.4, respectively.

Once an individual begins collecting Social Security, there is no endpoint. In other words, if you live to be 150, you can still collect based on your original contributions. Hence the future projected stress on the current Social Security surplus.

This projected deficit doesn't mean that the Social Security reservoir will completely run dry, nor that the Social Security Administration will not be able to pay all claimants. It only means that with a declining reservoir level not all claimants will have their full demands met. So some type of rationing will be forced. *If nothing is done,* at most the federal government will only be able to pay 77 cents on the dollar, not an insignificant amount.

What does this mean? Say you have accumulated $300,000 in Social Security benefits during your working life. These are *your* benefits that *you* worked hard for and in the absence of the Social Security program you might have accrued it in higher wages, and or as another benefit. But with a projected drop in the reservoir (due to greater life expectancy) the best the government can do is to pay you 77 cents on the dollar. This means that rather than receiving your full $300,000, you only would receive only $231,000, a substantial reduction. But what happened to the $69,000 that is rightfully yours? Just like a declining reservoir, some of the water, but not all, has disappeared and cannot be used. If nothing is done, this "water" will be gone. Hence the need to do something now.

Wait a minute you might say, why can't I earmark my tax contributions right now for *my* exclusive use when I retire? Not a bad idea, but that's not how the Social Security system works. When Social Security was being discussed during the 1930s, the Roosevelt administration rejected this idea in favor of the current system (also known as pay as you go), in which current contributors fund current users with any leftovers funding a general surplus. Roosevelt, worried that his landmark legislation would be dismantled by a future administration, felt that this was the only way to institutionalize Social Security and give it some permanence. In other words, if I make contributions now, but today's beneficiaries are currently using *my* contributions, then it has to keep going so that it can pay me *my* benefits when I need them. So, it is in *my* best interest not to dismantle the program or allow anyone else to do so. In this respect Roosevelt was right, and this is the main reason why there is visceral opposition across party lines to any talk of dismantling the current OASDI.

Social Security, created by the Social Security Act of 1935, is the largest source of government spending, accounting for one out of five dollars spent, and it is the second largest source of federal government revenue, accounting for just over one out of every three dollars received. (I discuss government finances in more depth in chapter 10.)

Social Security is funded by a 6.2 percent tax on wages earned, matched by a 6.2 percent tax on the employer. (If you are self-employed then your share is doubled.) Only wages are taxed, so if you earn your living by collecting rent, interest, or profits, your income is exempt from Social Security taxation. Currently the maximum ceiling for wages taxed is $147,000, which increases annually by the rate of inflation as does the level of benefits.

Social Security checks are directly linked to inflation via a cost-of-living adjustment (COLA). In 2023, Social Security checks will increase by 8.79 percent, the largest increase since 1981's increase of 11.2 percent. This higher COLA will in turn boost the average monthly Social

Security check from $1,669 today to $1,814 in 2023. The maximum taxable wage will increase from today's $147,000 to $160,200 in 2023.[2]

The increase in monthly checks will be welcomed news for most social security beneficiaries, although certainly not all, "since more people will owe federal income tax on their Social Security benefits, since the $25,000 income threshold for individuals, or $32,000 for couples, isn't adjusted for inflation". The higher Social Security payments will add to the fiscal stress of the federal government, pushing forward the expected date of the transition of the Social Security surplus into a deficit by one year from 2035 to 2034.[3]

Currently there are 70 million Social Security recipients. Today, approximately 90 percent of Americans, age sixty-five and older receive Social Security benefits, accounting for 30 percent of their total income on average.[4]

Saving Social Security

The past ten annual Social Security reports (published by the Social Security Administration) have warned that the OASDI surplus will dry up. So, this year's report is nothing new. The reports have sparked dialogue about various solutions ranging from sun-setting the program (letting it run out and fade away) to raising OASDI taxes, reducing benefits, increasing the ceiling on wages, and levying the Social Security tax on all forms of income (rent, profits, interest) rather than just wages. Since 2035 is in the distant congressional future, it has invited more inaction than action.

Each of these solutions (including inaction, which is a solution, albeit a poor one) will create more problems than it will solve. Why should overburdened Americans pay more Social Security taxes? And why should we give up any more of our hard-earned wages? My policies will increase the labor force and, coupled with my immigration reform, will result in more people working. So even if the Social Security tax rate does not change (and there is no reason that it should), the reservoir level will rise.

The main lever connecting the inflow and the outflow of the Social Security reservoir is the number of workers. Just like a reservoir, if the inflow relative to the outflow decreases, the water level falls. This makes it more difficult to maintain the outflow; and making it difficult, if not impossible, to satisfy the demands of all reservoir users. Since every additional labor force participant earning wages pays taxes, more labor force participants will, all else equal, increase Social Security's current surplus.

Medicare Trouble

Medicare, the second largest federal government spending item, was established in 1965 along with Medicaid as an amendment to the 1935 Social Security Act. It provides health care insurance for Americans over the age of sixty-five. Medicaid, the fifth largest government program, provides health care insurance for the indigent, and is funded by general tax revenue from both the federal and local governments.

Medicare similarly works like a reservoir: the inflow is contributed by those of us working, with the outflow paying for health insurance in one way or another for people over the age of sixty-five.

Medicare is divided into several parts:

- Part A: Hospital Insurance.

- Part B: Supplementary Medical Insurance.

- Part C: An additional insurance option for people who are eligible for Medicare.

- Part D: New drug program.

Currently Part A is in surplus, but its projected surplus will disappear in 2028—a lot sooner than Social Security. This is due to Americans living longer *and* to increasing medical care costs. Older Americans have a greater demand for health care. The greater life expectancy, the greater the demand. Parts B and D are currently in deficit with payroll taxes and premiums only covering 57 percent of the benefits.

The depletion of the current surplus does not mean that Part A will be fully depleted or that the fund will go bankrupt, only that that the promised benefits will not materialize on the dollar. Like Social Security, various solutions are being discussed, such as reducing benefits and increasing taxes. But if my policies are implemented, there is no need for such disruptions. As the labor force increases, more workers will contribute tax revenue to the Medicare Trust Fund.

Conclusion

The importance of Social Security for most Americans and hence the importance of my policies is evidenced by the fact that few Americans have a pension, and few have managed to save enough for retirement, so there is an overreliance on Social Security.[5] While this situation is certainly not ideal and was not envisioned by the architects of Social Security (they assumed retirees would also access their savings along with a pension) it is currently a fact of life, which gives an added sense of urgency to the necessity of implementing my plan.

The reason for the projected Social Security and Medicare deficit is that we are living longer. Rather than raising taxes or reducing benefits my policies will, by increasing the labor force, keep the surplus intact.

CHAPTER 7

Reducing the Deficit and Debt

George Washington—a hero of the Revolutionary War, enshrined on Mt. Rushmore, on the face of the US one dollar bill—was very much revered as America's first president except for one thing: budget deficits. Even Washington's relatives got on his case for not balancing the budget in five of his eight years, for not giving adequate attention to the budget problem.

**MY TWO-CENTS PLAN
ON THE DEFICIT AND THE DEBT**

Increase federal revenue while lowering taxation rates by incentivizing work and encouraging *legal* immigration.

Washington's immediate successors, John Adams and Thomas Jefferson, were more successful, only running budget deficits in two of their collective twelve years. In fact, throughout the nineteenth century and continuing to the beginning of the Great Depression in 1930, the American government was fairly successful at balancing its budget: running deficits in only 30 percent of the years. Of those years, 30 percent were during wartime. Regardless of the political party, it was assumed that the federal government should conduct its finances no differently than an ordinary business: be frugal, prudent, and avoid unnecessary spending. War was the only exception.

From 1865 to 1893, the federal government set a record for the most consecutive years (twenty-eight) running a budget surplus. It is a safe bet that this record will not be broken, at least in the near term.[1]

Fast-forward to the modern era. From 1931 to 2022, the federal government ran budget deficits in 92 percent of the years. Since 1960, the years of budget surpluses are so few and far between that one can easily recite them: 1960, 1969, and 1997-2001. Mirroring the nineteenth century record for budget surpluses, from 1970 to 1996, the federal government posted the longest era of consecutive budget deficits, although the current string of consecutive deficits (2002- ?) will give the record a run for its money.

So what happened in the 1930s to change the budget mindset? Firstly, a revolution in economic thinking. We started assuming that not only is deficit spending OK, but it is the only way to jump-start an economy stuck in a recession (the unemployment rate reached a record 24.9 percent in 1933 and continued in double digits until 1940). Second, a massive increase in federal spending from 1938 through 1945, which, in effect, ended the Great Depression and, at least at the time, gave credence to the belief that fiscal spending can "solve" a depression. These two elements (the necessity of federal deficit spending and active fiscal spending) formed the crux of Keynesian economics, which Milton Friedman and others have rebelled against (see chapter 10).[2]

Today's Deficits/Debt

Today's deficits are much larger than in the past in terms of absolute numbers (See Figure 7.1.) Notice the sharp increase after 9/11, and after the recessions of 2007-2009 and 2020.

In 2021, with federal government revenue at $4.05 trillion and federal government spending at $6.82 trillion, the deficit was $2.75 trillion.

According to the Congressional Budget Office (July 2022, Table C-1, 55) the federal deficit as a percent of GDP is currently at 3.54 percent and, unless nothing is done, is expected to steadily increase to 6.3 percent in 2033, and then to 10.8 percent by 2051. The reason, as will be explained later in this chapter and in the next, is excessive spending.[3]

Figure 7.1 USA federal budget deficits since 2000

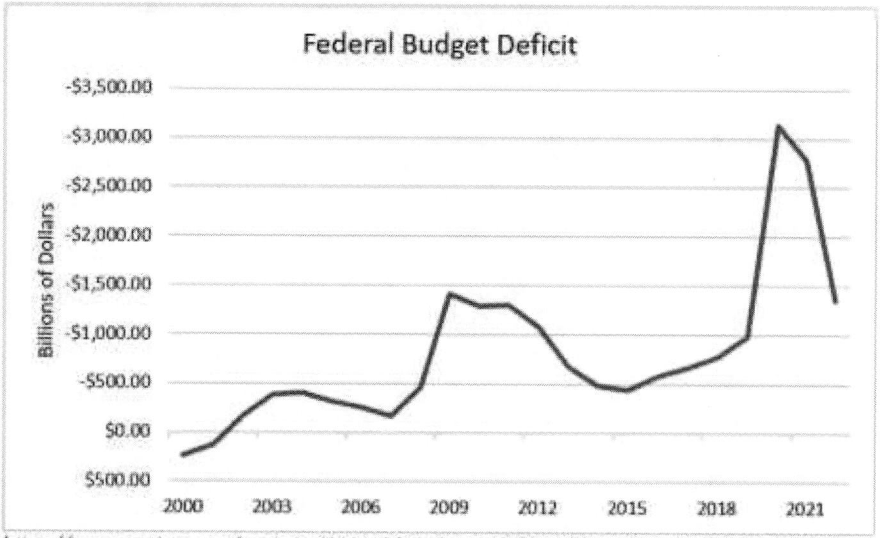

Federal Budget Deficit

Like anyone who spends more than one receives in income, he or she must borrow to cover the difference, which is exactly what is happening in the USA. Figure 7.2 charts the total federal debt since 1981.[4] Between 1980 and 1981, the total federal debt crossed the psychological threshold of $1 trillion in nominal terms (i.e., the actual prices of the day). Since 1980 the nominal debt has increased thirty-fold. As of October 2022, our total (or gross) federal debt-to-GDP ratio is 125.55 percent, which means if we wanted to pay off our debt completely, we could use every dollar of income that Americans earned in one year, but then we would need to come up with an additional amount (25.55

percent of GDP). Needless to say, we do not ever want to be in a situation where we must immediately pay off our federal debt.

Andrew Jackson, during his second administration (1832–1836), was the only USA president to ever do so. But it set the stage for a painful recession for Jackson's successor (Martin Van Buren, Jackson's VP, who became president in 1836) since most of the debt-financing loans to the Treasury were made by Europeans. This meant that to repay the debt, money left the USA for Europe. The result was the devastating Panic of 1837.[5]

Figure 7.2: The USA federal debt since 1981

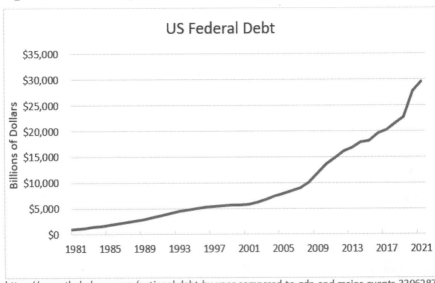

https://www.thebalance.com/national-debt-by-year-compared-to-gdp-and-major-events-3306287

Perhaps a more apropos measure is the debt held by the public as a percentage of GDP (federal debt/GDP) (see Figure 7.3).[6] A nation's GDP represents the market value of all goods and services produced within its borders in one year; but at the same time, it also represents the income of everyone producing that output. Just like if you go to the bank and ask for a loan, the first question the banker will ask is your income. That, in effect, is what the debt-to–GDP ratio tells us: the debt accumulated by the federal government to pay for its deficits divided by the earned income of all Americans in one year.

According to the Congressional Budget Office (July 2022) this ratio crossed 100 percent in 2021 (a historic high). After dipping slightly in 2022 and 2023, it is expected to steadily increase, reaching 180 percent by 2051. Yes, that is right! 180 percent! Unless, of course, something is done to reverse this explosive growth.

Figure 7.3 The Federal Debt Held by the Public as a Percent of GDP

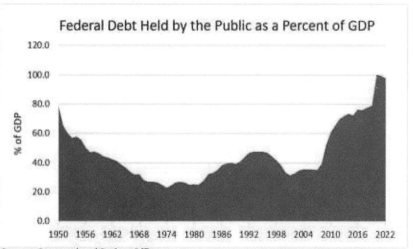

Source: Congressional Budget Office

Should we worry about the Debt?

Former Chairman of the Joint Chiefs of Staff Admiral Mike Mullen has repeatedly declared "the most significant threat to our national security is our debt."[7] Based on my causal talking with Americans, the explosion of debt is most worrisome. Will we be able to pay it back? Why are we unfairly burdening our grandchildren? According to the Committee for a Responsible Budget we have several reasons to worry about the federal debt:

- **Rising debt slows income growth**: According to the CBO, each $1 of new borrowing reduces total investment by 33 cents, with 24 cents shifted to foreigners who will benefit from America's largesse. With rising debt, investors will purchase debt at the expense of private investment. The Committee predicts that if the public debt as a percent of GDP reaches 150 percent in 2050 as projected, individual income will decrease by 6 percent.

- **Rising interest rates are becoming more important**: Currently, net interest on the federal debt is at 1.4 percent of GDP and is projected to increase to 3.0 percent of GDP in 2029, and 6.3 percent by 2050. Interest payments will be the fastest increasing part of the federal budget.

  "Over time, interest spending will eclipse spending on other programs. Under current law, interest payments on the debt will exceed the cost of Medicaid by 2020 and spending on defense by 2025, and it will be the single largest government expenditure after 2050. Framed a different way, interest payments already consume every dollar raised by the corporate income tax, the estate tax, gift taxes, and federal excise taxes. By the late 2040s, under current law interest costs will consume all payroll tax revenue.... [This means that] every dollar spent on interest is a dollar unavailable for something else.[8]"

- **Rising debt causes underlying interest rates to rise**: As more government debt is issued, investors demand higher interest rates to compete with other investment opportunities. One study found that for each 10 percent of GDP increase in the national debt, interest rates increase by 0.2-0.3 percentage points.[9]

- The higher the debt, the more politically and economically difficult it is to borrow money to fight future crises (if indeed borrowing money is our goal, which it should not be).

- **Rising debt increasingly burdens future generations:** "The federal government is projected to spend more on servicing its debt obligations than it does on all programs and funding for children. In other words, the government will spend more on funding the last generation's consumption than investing in the future."[10] In addition, slowing income, rising interest rates, and declining fiscal space will cumulatively affect future generations.

- **Rising debt increases the risk of a fiscal crisis:** especially if the underlying economic fundamentals worsen. This might cause investors to pull out their money or demand higher interest rates.

The Committee for a Responsible Budget Concludes:

Rather than putting our national and economic security further at risk and enhancing the negative consequences of borrowing by adding more to the debt, policymakers should pay for new proposals and come together on policies to improve our fiscal situation. Without a solution, the consequences of debt will gradually worsen over time and may be difficult to reverse.[11]

I could not agree more. After all, this is what my policies are all about.

How to Reduce the Deficit

The budget is a relationship between revenue and spending. You do not need to be a rocket scientist to understand that a deficit occurs if we spend too much vis-à-vis revenue. Or that the only way to reduce a deficit is to cut spending and increase revenue via economic growth.

Central to my policies is a highly achievable plan to increase the labor force participation rate and to welcome more *legal* immigrants to our shores. By bringing in more workers, my policies will enlarge the taxpaying base. With a higher LFPR, the poverty rate will decrease, as will means-test budgetary items, both discretionary and non-discretionary, especially Medicaid.

Thus, my policies will directly increase federal revenue without increasing the rate of taxation, and it will indirectly reduce government spending. As I will discuss in chapter 10, I also want to reduce and streamline the current USA tax structure. By reducing discretionary spending across the board by 2 percent, economic growth will increase, as will entrepreneurial activity and productivity. Budget revenue will increase. This will happen while we are also reducing and streamlining the current tax code (see chapter 10). My policies will not only reduce the current budget deficit, but they will reduce the federal debt by running budget surpluses.[12]

CHAPTER 8

Reducing Discretionary Spending

A central element of my Two-Cents plan is to reduce discretionary spending annually by 2 percent across the board. The money saved will be directly returned to the American taxpayers. Not only will this reduce government overgrowth, but it will clear the way for more productive growth in the private sector—the true source of wealth. I am not advocating for the abolition of government, nor the abolition of any particular government program, just the fruitful (and long overdue) paring of choking overgrowth.

> **MY TWO-CENTS PLAN**
> **ON DISCRETIONARY SPENDING**
>
> **Reduce discretionary spending across the board by 2 percent while towing the line on non-discretionary spending.**

All western nations have experienced a steady increase in government spending, and the USA is no exception (see Figure 8.1). Rising from about 10 percent of GDP in 1870, it is now about 39 percent and is expected to continue increasing. (More on this later in the chapter.)

Figure 8.1 USA federal government spending as a percent of GDP

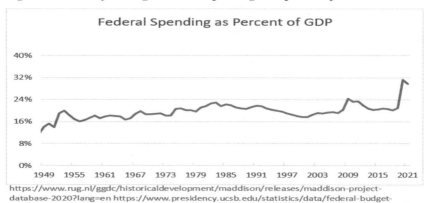

https://www.rug.nl/ggdc/historicaldevelopment/maddison/releases/maddison-project-
database-2020?lang=en https://www.presidency.ucsb.edu/statistics/data/federal-budget-
receipts-and-outlays https://www.whitehouse.gov/omb/budget/historical-tables/
https://www.usinflationcalculator.com/inflation/historical-inflation-rates/

As the USA becomes more affluent, we demand more social goods like education and environmental spending. As we live longer, we demand more health care and social security. But this does not give us a carte blanche for continued expansion of government programs, nor does it mean that continued unopposed government growth is either necessary or productive. As I mentioned in the previous chapter, the USA is deep in debt and cannot afford *any more!*

Unfortunately, once enacted, government programs continue in motion, expanding, getting more clout and more resources, further increasing leverage, and preventing any opposition from materializing. Defending the turf and expanding becomes the modus operandi. No graph better illustrates this than Figure 8.2, which includes both discretionary and mandatory spending.[1]

Figure 8.2 USA Annual Federal Spending

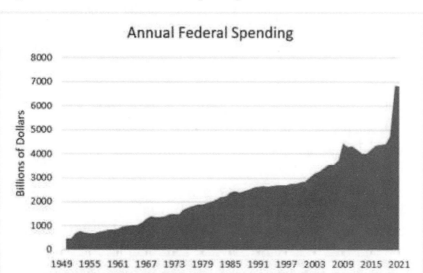

Source: Historical Tables, Budget of the United States Government

I am not sure about you, but I've yet to come across a government agency actively clamoring for fewer funds. Let me tell you a story. I started my business with a 110-square-foot office. I had only one employee—my secretary—which meant I was working long hours, seven days a week. As word of my business spread, the Navy contacted me to see if I could implement Statistical Process Control in their Naval supply centers and wanted to know what it would cost. I thought of the biggest number I could think of: "$100,000 should do the trick." The Navy spokesperson laughed that there was no way I could do the job for such a low sum. Not sure how to react, I offered $200,000. The same reaction. Then, $300,000. Identical reaction. We finally 'settled' at $400,000 along with a supplemental payment. This was both a training initiative and a software development initiative. They were correct because the government moves at a very slow pace. In addition, there are so many people that must be sold on every little thing that is done that it is extremely costly and time consuming. But it did teach me an awful lot about the cost of a huge bureaucracy. In fairness, in the private sector I could have probably implemented this for $100,000, whereas in this government contract I may have actually lost money. It was well worth any loss or expenditures, however, because of the insight I got into the difficulties in trying to change cemented ideas and approaches in a bureaucratic environment.

The lesson that I immediately learned (and there is a lot more where these came from) was that government agencies must spend their allocated budget every year. If not, next year's budget is reduced, thus forfeiting staff and prestige. As someone who has always been concerned about quality and controlling costs, I thought this was the nuttiest thing I had ever seen.

Imagine a private sector business operating this way? Or better yet, show me *one* private business that does. Few (if any) would ever survive with such a bloated, continuously expansive model. Whereas private businesses focus on creating value and maximizing profit, the typical government agency lobbies for continued spending and enlarging its budget, while ignoring the source of funding—namely the American taxpayer—and pushing for greater control over our own money.

One of the reasons I am so effective at controlling costs is that I have done so all my life. Even though I had a wonderful childhood, my parents did not have much money. They certainly did not have enough to pay for college. To attend, I had to come up with the money myself. In the summer I worked at the steel mill and at Lieber Brothers Corporation as a laborer. At the time I thought they were paying me what seemed like a fortune. I was making about $140.00 per week. I saved all the money and of course this was enough to sustain me. In the middle of my junior and senior years in college I played a lot of poker and ended up in good shape financially. In fact, I thought I was loaded. I was even able to lend my parents money. Graduate school was substantially different, however. There was a time when I was in abysmal financial shape. Things were so bad that I was receiving eviction notices and even had my electricity shut off.

My most frightening experience is something that I will remember forever. I was given an eviction notice and had to come up with $1,300 in two days. A gentleman who owned a couple of clinics had wanted to play me in a bridge game. I had been so busy that I really had not had any time before but now it had become a necessity. My best friend, Michael, was in med school and was equally broke, so we arranged the bridge game. Fortunately, I won $1,300 and was able to avoid eviction. I know what it is like to not have money for food and to not pay the rent. These are things you never forget; they stay with you for life. I can empathize with the average family suffering under the exorbitantly high prices of gas, food, and housing. Having suffered through tough economic hardships in my early days, I learned some life-long lessons, especially the value of the dollar and what it means to earn an income and to pay for things oneself, without incurring any debt. My early life experiences made me very cautious in my spending habits. I have no personal debt, no mortgage and none of my seventy-eight companies has any debt or have ever filed for bankruptcy. If any of my companies ever need money, I fund them myself.

In contrast, the federal government has been increasing its spending and regulations for decades. Since 1970 the number of federal regulations here in the USA has doubled (see Figure 8.3).

Figure 8.3 The growth in the pages of federal regulations since 1950

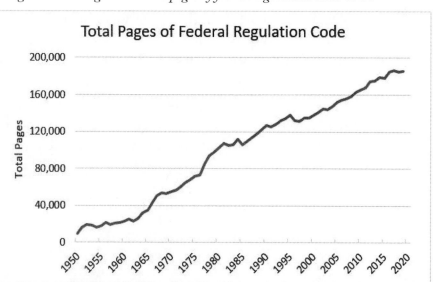

https://regulatorystudies.columbian.gwu.edu/reg-stats

The federal government has infiltrated every part of our economy from occupational licensing to unneeded regulations on oil and gas drilling. While the leftist liberals argue that our economy needs *more* regulations, the truth is just the opposite: we need *less*—a lot less. Like weeds choking a garden, government spending and government regulations are overgrown. A trim is long overdue. With the excessive regulations, growing debt, and federal spending out of control (see chapter 9), it's no wonder US productivity has been in the doldrums.

We have come to rely on government spending as the only solution to any and every problem. Like a baseball pitcher relying on one pitch, assuming it should be used against every hitter in every situation or a golfer assuming only one club should be used in every situation—short putts or long drives—we have become accustomed to using only one instrument (the federal government) and assuming it can solve every problem.

My plan is all about recognizing that we have used only a limited number of clubs in the bag, and that we have a lot more in our repertoire. Let's be creative, America, in how we conceptualize our problems and how we solve them. Needless to say, creating more government programs, adding more stimuli, *not* reducing inflation, and paying people not to work *is not* the way to go!

The American taxpayer needs to take back control over how our tax dollars are spent, who spends them, and for what purpose. We need to rescue our economy before it becomes fully overgrown with the choking weeds of government. We must incentivize people to work by reducing their rates of taxation while also removing all disincentives to work (see chapter 3).

Cartoon 18 – Biden's Unemployment

My plan will unleash market forces, achieve a more sustainable use of fossil fuels, and reduce inflation. By incentivizing a more active and productive labor force, my plan will promote economic growth, ease the demand for means-tested programs, reduce the deficit, and shore up Social Security and Medicare.

Discretionary Spending

Discretionary spending is implemented annually through an appropriations bill by Congress. The federal government must vote and agree on the exact levels of spending. Discretionary spending includes defense, education, transportation, energy, NASA, homeland security, the War on Terror, along with thousands of individual programs. If the government wanted to (or perhaps better stated, if the government could agree) it could effectively reduce the budget of a discretionary program to zero.

Compare this to non-discretionary spending, which is created by an act of Congress and cannot be changed (along with its specified level of benefits) without another act of Congress. Such programs are also called mandatory since the federal government *must* annually allocate the necessary funds to keep them running. Congress can reduce funding only on a discretionary program by changing the authorization law, which requires sixty votes in the Senate.

National defense has historically formed the largest component of discretionary spending.[2] The reason: defending the nation has long been considered federal government's preponderant goal. Take it from Adam Smith himself, the founding father of economics: "The first duty of the sovereign, that of protecting the society from the violence and invasion of other independent societies, can be performed only by means of military force."[3]

Unless you have been living on Mars the last few years, you would know that discretionary spending has steadily (and inexorably) increased since 1950 (see Figure 8.4).

Figure 8.4 The level of discretionary spending, 1950-2022

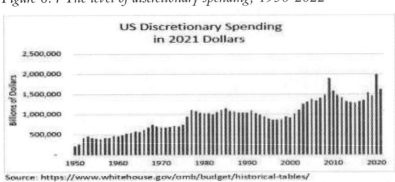

From 2019 to 2020 we saw the largest increase ever in discretionary spending from $1.34 trillion to $1.63 trillion, a whopping 22 percent increase. As a percent of GDP, discretionary spending increased by 24 percent from 2019 to 2020: from 6.3 percent of GDP in 2019 to 7.8 percent of GDP 2020; the latter being the highest level since 2012. Figure 8.5 gives a good indication of the size of the major categories of discretionary spending.

Figure 8.5 Discretionary Spending Breakdown

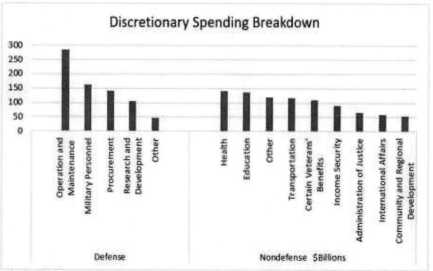

Source: CBO

As a percent of total government spending, discretionary spending has steadily decreased to its current level of 35 percent, while non-discretionary spending, as a percent of total spending, has steadily increased. Figure 8.6 shows the historical levels of discretionary spending versus non-discretionary spending:

Figure 8.6 Discretionary versus non-discretionary spending

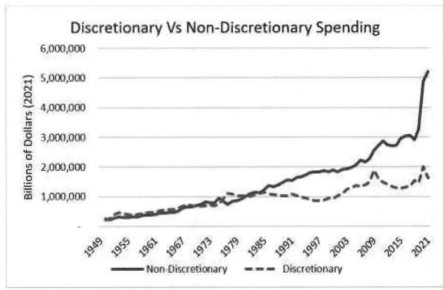

https://www.whitehouse.gov/omb/budget/historical-tables/

My plan will reduce discretionary spending by 2 percent across the board. In addition, for every government agency that reduces spending by 2 percent, its manager would receive a portion of the savings with the remainder returned to the American taxpayers. This way, everyone wins, and especially ordinary Americans.

In my experience there are three things that effectively motivate job performance: money, praise, and recognition. No matter what anyone says, money is paramount. My office employees, for example, all earn a bonus to reward their performance.

Figure 8.7 shows the effect on the federal deficit of reducing discretionary spending by 2 percent across the board *without* considering any other of my policies. Keep in mind that these other effects are mutually reinforcing, so once implemented we would expect a much quicker attainment of a balanced budget and even a budget surplus.

Figure 8.7 The federal deficit with a 2 percent annual reduction in discretionary spending

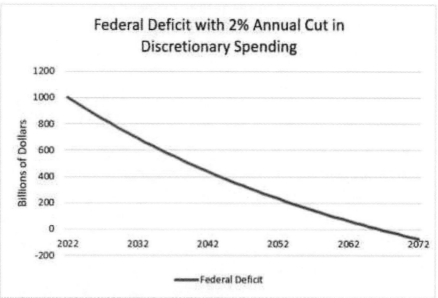

Note: A balanced budget is reached by 2067. This graph assumes all other deficit variables are held constant. A deficit of $1 trillion is the baseline deficit.

Non-Discretionary Spending

The main non-discretionary programs are Social Security, Medicare, and Medicaid. These three mandatory programs account for one-third of total government spending and 50 percent of total mandatory spending! With Social Security coming on board in 1935, and Medicare/Medicaid in 1965, we can begin to understand the recent explosion in mandatory spending.

With Americans living longer, and health care costs continuing to increase, expect non-discretionary spending, both absolutely and as a percent of total spending, to continue to increase (see Figure 8.8).

Figure 8.8 The level of non-discretionary spending 1950-2022

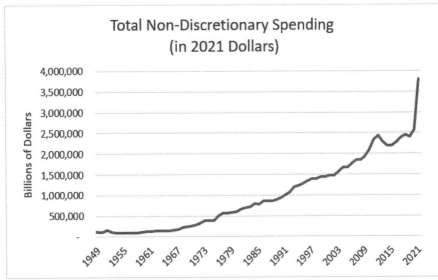

https://www.whitehouse.gov/omb/budget/historical-tables/

Interest on the federal debt is officially its own category, separate from discretionary and non-discretionary spending. But since the exact amount of interest must be paid when due (or the government declares bankruptcy), it technically becomes part of mandatory spending. Currently at $305 billion, and as explained in the previous chapter, the interest on the federal debt is the fastest growing federal expense, and if nothing is done, the Congressional Budget Office expects it to triple by 2051, reaching a tad under $1 trillion dollars. Wow!

Conclusion

Being elected to government demands accountability to its citizens—a bedrock principle of any democracy. But our suffocating government has weakened and obfuscated this critical link. By trimming the fat from every discretionary program and returning the money directly to the American people, my policies will clear the overgrown brush and restore this crucial lifeline between the government and its people. In so doing, my policies will jump-start our economy by incentivizing work, thereby adding to government revenue, and reducing means-tested spending.

CHAPTER 9

Boosting Productivity

J ust when I thought I had heard all the Biden bad news, the Bureau of Labor Statistics (BLS) reported that in the second quarter of 2022 productivity decreased 4.1 percent from the previous quarter (See Figure 9.1). This follows a 7.4 percent decrease in productivity in the first quarter of 2021 from the last quarter of 2021. Get this: From the second quarter of 2021 to the second quarter of 2022, productivity decreased by 2.4 percent, the largest decline since data was first collected in 1948.[1]

**MY TWO-CENTS PLAN
ON PRODUCTIVITY**

Reverse the current unacceptable decline in productivity and hence living standards with specific policies to incentivize work.

As a businessperson and as an American I am baffled and aghast by this news. The productivity of my employees is key to *our* success. If they produce nothing, then there is no output and no profits, and hence nothing for wages. The more they produce the greater the output. With more output per employee, my unit labor costs decrease, which in turn increases profits.[2] In addition, higher wages enable me to attract the best talent without increasing prices, which further boosts productivity, and so on. Higher productivity means we all benefit; it is what unites us as a business.

Figure 9.1 Change in USA productivity

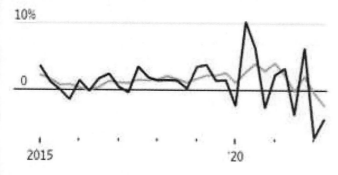

U.S. nonfarm labor productivity, change from prior quarter

■ Quarterly ■ 4-quarter average

Note: Seasonally adjusted annual rate
Source: Labor Department

As productivity increases so does the overall standard of living. This is how it was for the generation immediately after World War II, when productivity increased at an annual rate of 2.8 percent between 1947-1973. Middle-class workers earned a decent living, they lived in a nice suburban house, and sent their kids to college.[3] Higher productivity provided businesses a substantial cushion to boost wages. It was no coincidence that inflation during this period was mostly a non-issue (except for the late 1960s due to increased Vietnam War spending and LBJ's War on Poverty). The pie was growing, and everyone was able to get a bigger piece of a growing pie. This was the golden age for the American middle class.

With productivity increasing at 2.8 percent annually, living standards were doubling every twenty-five years. Americans rightfully felt that they were living better than their parents, and that the living standards of their children would be better than theirs. This is what the American Dream is all about.

But then America got hit with higher oil prices, along with the recessions of 1973-1975, 1980, and 1981-1982. Thanks to economic mismanagement, America simultaneously experienced a new phenomenon: inflation and unemployment (i.e., stagflation).[4] During those tough economic times, productivity only managed to increase by 1.6 percent per annum. Then after briefly spiking upwards at a 2.8 percent annually (from 1998-2008) in large part thanks to the evolution of the internet productivity fell back to its present pace of only 1.5 percent per annum (See Figure 9.2).

Figure 9.2 Changes in post-WWII USA productivity

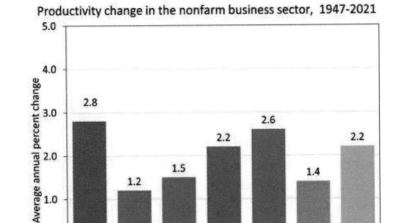

Labor force shortages, supply-side bottlenecks, sluggish demand, intrusive energy regulations, and the longest recession (2007-2009) since the Great Depression have kept us in the productivity doldrums, increasing at 1.8 percent per annum, which, in turn, has generated consternation among economists and public policy officials.

What is Productivity? How is it Measured?

The Bureau of Labor Statistics (BLS) officially defines and calculates USA productivity. Accordingly, productivity, or output per hour, is calculated by dividing an index of real output [real GDP] by an index of hours worked for all persons, including employees, proprietors, and unpaid family workers," measuring, in effect how much output a worker produces while ignoring how much the worker *can* produce and the quality of that output. [5] Sounds rather blunt and even simplistic. And in a way it is.. If the inputs can be used in such a way that more output can be produced, then the inputs are said to be more productive. The more output for a given level of resources, the greater the productivity and vice versa.

Productivity can increase due to more and better labor, more and better capital, and the right mixing between the these "raw" ingredients.[6] These factors can and often do reinforce each other. For example, better-trained workers can more effectively utilize better capital and vice versa.[7] Just like a chef whipping up a soufflé, we start with the basic ingredients and the better the quality, the better tasting the dish. The basic ingredients are of course necessary but not sufficient. You need the acumen, the know-how of *how* to mix the ingredients together in a specific order and a specific proportion. Otherwise, the raw ingredients, no matter how good, will sit there like lumpy raisins in a fruitcake.[8]

The central point is that productivity is a fraction with a numerator and denominator. So mathematically if the numerator decreases so does productivity, all else equal. If the denominator increases so does productivity, all else equal. This is exactly what happened in 2022: Real GDP (the numerator) declined by 1.6 percent in the first quarter of and by 0.6 percent in the second quarter. Likewise, in the second quarter, hours worked increased 2.7 percent from the first quarter. This is on top of a 4.2 percent increase from the last quarter of 2021 to the first quarter of 2022.

Cartoon 19 – Digging for Gold

In essence, workers are working more and producing less, while the economy is contracting, and inflation is increasing. To top this off, inflation has reduced workers' real compensation by 4.4 percent from the second quarter of 2021 to the second quarter of 2022.

Yeah, a lot of statistics here, but the bottom line is that our current predicament is unprecedented, at least in modern times, and at least since the BLS began collecting data. Obviously, this deplorable situation cannot continue. The most likely scenario is that firms will release workers, increasing the unemployment rate. How much so is anyone's guess right now. Another scenario is that the "excess" workers can be retained, but only by passing on the costs to customers. But this assumes that customers will pay for the added costs, and that the Federal Reserve will stand idly by. It is unrealistic to assume either.

In a surprisingly candid statement, Shawn Sprague, a BLS productivity economist, wrote in *The Monthly Labor Review* (the flagship journal of the BLS) that

> Not only has the productivity slowdown been one of the most consequential economic phenomena of the last two decades, but it also represents the most profound economic mystery during this time, and though many economists have grappled with this issue for over a decade and even created some innovative research... we still cannot fully explain what brought on this situation.[9]

Perhaps one reason that economists cannot fully explain productivity is the difficulty distinguishing between the long-run trend (productivity has languished since 2005) from the short-term effects (e.g., the COVID effects with the resulting layoffs, remote work, longer hours). Obviously the short- and long-term factors mutually interact. Nevertheless, I see nothing that the Biden administration has done to reverse the long-term trend. Rather his policies have exacerbated it.

My Policies Will Increase Productivity

Increasing productivity across the board is absolutely essential. It is a key solution for inflation and an affordable way out of our energy conundrum. Increasing productivity via innovations and hard work has been central in every energy revolution.[10] Spurred by the possibility of monetary gain, individuals were (and are) self-motivated to pursue fame and fortune. By the way, increasing productivity is the key solution for stagflation.[11]

My policies will reverse this deplorable decline in productivity by incentivizing the private sector to innovate. This is a good example of Adam Smith's invisible hand at work: have the government step back, reduce regulations and tax rates, put more money into the hands of Americans (which was rightfully theirs in the first place), and let the market system do what it does best: innovate.

A defining feature of capitalism, at least the capitalism that I am familiar with, is incentivizing the will to innovate and experiment, thereby unleashing the spirt of entrepreneurialism without any directive from the federal government. The Biden administration, however, has extirpated this will, this spirit of American capitalism, and my policies will help resuscitate it.

Remember our discussion of the California Gold Rush? While the miners flocked to California in search of fortune, so did entrepreneurs. John Studebaker (of automobile fame) began his career by first selling wheelbarrows to the miners. As a teenager, Philip Armour began by selling meat to the miners. Henry Wells and William Fargo set up much-needed banking services for the miners. The German emigrant Levi Strauss, noticing that the arduous work took a toll on miners' pants, devised a tougher pair of overalls that would withstand the day-to-day mining rigors. Made from a blue cloth (called serge) from Nimes, France, Strauss' popular pants quickly alliterated into "denim."

American history is filled with such examples. This is what capitalism is all about. Understanding changing needs, innovating, and experimenting, and then inventing/offering something of value is the American way, the crux of the American Dream.

So, how best to nurture and cultivate this American Dream? Isn't the answer obvious? Encourage and incentivize inventors and entrepreneurs to do what they do best—innovate—while reducing government overreach and intrusive regulations.

My policies reduce discretionary spending by 2 percent across the board, increase the labor force participation rate, eliminate unnecessary government regulations on oil and natural gas, encourage legal immigration, all of which will unleash the entrepreneurial spirit and boost productivity. It will help our economy and America get back on track.

CHAPTER 10

Simplifying the US Tax Code

A dam Smith, founder of the discipline of economics, advocated a market system (i.e., capitalism) as being the most effective to generate wealth.[1] Contrary to the dominant thinking in his day, Smith argued that wealth is not a function of the amount of gold or silver a nation possesses, but how well off each individual is. This is important, because for Smith (and for us) a nation can only be wealthy if all its citizens are able to adequately provision. Smith also argued that capitalism's wealth-creating ability is not a zero-sum game, that is, my creating wealth does not detract from society's wealth, but instead adds to it, making everyone better off.

Smith did not call for an abolition of government, for that would be anarchy; instead, he called for government support of the crucial pillars of capitalism such as the protection of property rights, the provision of public goods such as national defense, and basic education.

MY TWO CENTS
ON TAX RATES

Reduce income tax rates across the board while reducing the number of tax brackets.

Unfortunately, the disciplines of economics and politics do not offer us a prescriptive rule for the ideal government involvement in a market system. Indeed, the history of capitalism oscillates between extensive government intervention (during the 1930s and the 1960s, for example) and a more hands-off laissez-faire (most of the nineteenth century and the 1980s) approach. My position, as I have argued throughout this book, is that our government has overextended itself and that we need less government and not more.

How does the government get its revenue?

Governments can fund spending by printing money, taxing citizens, and borrowing from the public. While all three methods have been used in the US at one time or another, today's preponderant source of revenue is taxation, and specifically the income tax (See Figure 10.1).

Figure 10.1 Federal Government Revenue by Source, 2021

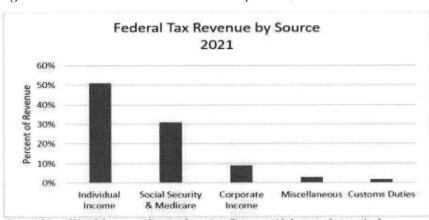

Source: https://datalab.usaspending.gov/americas-finance-guide/revenue/categories/

The income tax is progressive since as one's income increases so does the rate of taxation. While certainly not ideal, a progressive tax is considered by most Americans to be more equitable than a regressive tax (as one's income decreases so does the rate of taxation). The Social Security tax, the federal government's second largest source of revenue, is regressive[2] since everyone pays the same rate on income earned up until the $147,000 ceiling, when the tax rate effectively becomes zero.

A problem, of course, with any progressive tax is that it incentivizes behavioral changes. For example, if I receive a raise that pushes me into a higher tax bracket, I might divert my income into non-taxable sources. For this reason, some people call for a flat tax, also called a lump-sum tax. It levies the same percent tax on everyone regardless of income. (Although, a minimal income level is usually recognized. More on this later in this chapter.) While this solves the behavioral problem, it is seen as unfair by most of the American public, who believe that the rich should pay more. While I personally empathize with those who call for a flat tax, I do believe that the federal income tax should be progressive, although greatly simplified from its current form (see later in this chapter). It is hard for me to justify someone who spends 20 percent of their income for food paying the same tax rate as someone who spends less than 1 percent of their income for food.

The top marginal rates of taxation have varied considerably during American history from a high of 94 percent during WWII to 25 percent in 1925. A tax rate of 94 percent effectively means that for each additional dollar I earn, I keep $0.06 while giving the government $0.94. The disincentives are obvious. If everyone averts paying taxes due to its high level, then the government obviously doesn't receive any revenue.[3]

The Laffer Curve

Arthur Laffer famously sketched out on a napkin the above implicit relationship between the tax rate and the government's maximum level of collected revenue[4] (see Figure 10.2).

Figure 10.2: The Laffer Curve

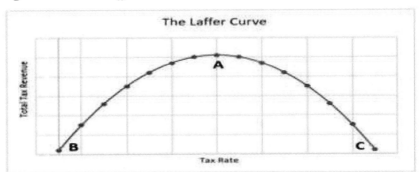

At the two endpoints (B and C) the collected revenue is zero, since a tax of 0 percent collects 0 revenue, as does a tax of 100 percent. (Why bother to work if one must give 100 percent of your income to the government?) Point A represents the maximum amount of revenue collected. If the government were to increase tax rates above this level, then total revenue would decrease; likewise, if the government reduces tax rates below this rate, revenue will also decrease.

Laffer's curve tells us that if tax rates are too high, and if the government reduces the rates of taxation, its revenue will increase as it edges closer to the optimal rate. This is the basis of supply-side economics,[5] which argues that lower tax rates and reduced government regulation (aided by free trade) will increase the supply of goods and result in lower prices. More specifically, the elements of supply-side economics[6] include

> sound money; free trade; less regulation; low, flat-rate taxes; and spending restraint, as the keys to real economic growth. These ideas are grounded in a classical economic analysis that understands that people adjust their behavior when the incentives change. Accordingly, the lower the regulatory and trade barriers, and the lower and flatter the tax rate, the greater the incentive to produce.[7]

Supply-side economics is a basic prescript for running a capitalist economy. It works, and I support it.

The main effect of reducing tax rates is economic growth. The reason is simple, but once understood, powerfully explanatory: 69 percent of USA output is bought by consumers, with the rest split between the government, businesses, and foreigners. So, anything that increases consumer income, all else equal, will boost consumption spending and hence overall economic activity. Higher consumption spending will boost investment, which in turn increases economic growth in a never- ending upward cycle. Conversely, anything that reduces consumer spending, such as higher tax rates, higher interest rates, or higher inflation (or with Bidenomics all three!), will reduce consumption spending and overall economic activity. Indeed, typically as consumer spending declines a recession usually follows.

Supply-Side Economics

Ronald Reagan took office in 1981 (having defeated Jimmy Carter and the independent John Anderson in the 1980 election) amidst high inflation, rising interest rates, energy insecurity, uncertainty, and angst about the future. Sound familiar? Perhaps not coincidentally, following a Democratic administration guilty of economic mismanagement the USA experienced its highest inflation during the period 1979-1981, with 1980 setting the single year record.

To solve inflation (literally, to wring it out of the economy) the Fed raised interest rates to record levels. Oil prices had earlier increased due to the Iranian Revolution and the Soviet invasion of Afghanistan. Mix these together and we got (not surprisingly) back-to-back recessions: 1980 and 1981-1982. Such recessions are rare in the USA. Usually caused by economic mismanagement, they signal that something is fundamentally wrong with our economy.

Reagan campaigned on a platform of supply-side economics. More specifically, he knew that reducing tax rates and government regulation would spur economic growth. He enacted two major pieces of legislation, both significantly reducing tax rates: The Economic Recovery Act of 1981 and the Tax Reform Act of 1986. The latter Act reduced the number of tax brackets to two: 28 percent and 15 percent. It also changed the corporate tax from 46 percent to 34 percent. The cumulative effect of these acts was to set in motion a vigorous economic recovery that, although briefly interrupted in 1991-1992, continued through 2001.

After peaking in 1982, the unemployment rate fell to 5.4 percent in 1989. Inflation, after reaching a record during the Carter years, fell to 4.7 percent in 1988. The average real income for Americans increased by 17 percent during Reagan's eight years—a laudatory achievement considering that average real incomes stagnated for most Americans during the 1970s. Federal tax revenue doubled from $517 billion in 1980 to $1,032 billion in 1989. Although the latter is significant in and of itself, we must add a two-point addendum:

- Following the Economic Recovery Tax Act of 1981, as revenue initially fell, the opposition Democrats negotiated tax increases (The Tax Equity and Fiscal Responsibility Act of 1982) followed by three additional tax increasing measures. Although individual income rates were not increased, these measures (e.g., depreciation, investment tax credits, interest exclusion, increases in Social Security payroll taxes, etc.) unnecessarily and unfortunately increased the overall tax burden of Americans. Sadly, and not unexpectedly, the opposition Democrats focused more on the declining revenue than on the growth-inducing features of the Reagan tax cuts.

- The budget deficit increased from $190 billion to $290 billion because overall spending increasing significantly. A central objective of Reaganomics was to increase defense spending to economically suffocate an increasingly moribund USSR, while significantly reducing non-defense spending. But due to the obduracy of the opposition Democrats, non-defense spending did not adequately decrease. The conservative group, The Other Half of History, note, "If non-defense spending had merely kept pace with inflation during the 1980s, instead of growing by leaps and bounds, the rapidly increasing tax revenues of that era would have paid for Reagan's defense buildup while virtually eliminating the budget deficit."[8]

As the Heritage Foundation writes:

By every measure of prosperity, Reaganomics worked. Some twenty million new jobs were created. Inflation was brought under control. And inflation-adjusted income rose for all segments of the population. Much of the credit for this spectacular economic performance goes to the 1981 Economic Recovery Act, which cut rates across the board for individuals and reduced the tax burden on business.[9]

Reaganomics worked, as Mr. Laffer himself explains:

In the roughly 30 years from the 1980s through the first decade of the new century, supply-side ideas contributed to the longest boom in United States history and an incredible transformation of the world economy. According to the National Bureau of Economic Research, 1982-1999 was one continuous mega-economic expansion. In fact, as it stretched into 2007, this 25-year boom saw a tripling in the net wealth of U.S. households and businesses from $20 trillion in 1981 to $60 trillion by 2007. When adjusted for inflation, more wealth was created in this 25-year boom than in the previous 200 years. This sustained economic growth is not only impressive on its own, but even more astonishing as it compares to the period immediately preceding it. In the 10 years from 1972- 1982, recessions were deep, and recoveries were short. In fact, throughout American history, the nation's economy has been in recession or depression roughly one-third of the time. But from 1981-2005, the annual growth rate of real gross domestic product (GDP) in the U.S. was 3.4 percent per year, and 4.3 percent per year during the 1983-1989 Reagan expansion alone.[10]

Summation

Supply-side economics worked once, and it will work again. Of course, we also must actively reduce federal spending, which my policies will do. Although my labor force and immigration policies will provide an additional revenue surge, which in turn will reduce means-tested spending, it is critically important to consistently and persistently reduce discretionary spending across the board.

I am happy to say that my plan is solidly grounded in the proven lessons of Reaganomics. Just to reiterate, I will:

- Reduce discretionary spending by 2 percent annually.

- Incentivize managers of government bureaucracies to do more with less by awarding a bonus if they meet the annual budget reduction.

- Reduce and simplify the tax brackets from seven to two.[11] The currently tax brackets are: 37 percent, 35 percent, 32 percent, 24 percent, 22 percent, 12 percent, and 10 percent. I propose to reduce them to 28 percent and 15 percent. By doing so, people at all income levels will be incentivized to work more.

- It is important to reverse the long-standing decline in the labor force participation rate. Giving people more of their money that they had rightfully earned is the best way to do so. The increase in the labor force will increase government revenue, which will reduce the budget deficit and put downward pressure on interest rates thereby stimulating entrepreneurial activity and investment.

Johnsonomics Is Better

Reminding me of Dickens' *Tale of Two Cities*, Trump's four years as president can be characterized as a Tale of Two Economies. Indeed, from January 2017 when he took office to December 2020, the macroeconomic numbers were pretty good, especially compared to Obama's second term when the annual change in real GDP averaged only 2.2 percent. Trump bested this in each of the first three years of his administration: 2.3 percent in 2017, 2.9 percent in 2018, and 2.3 percent in 2019. The poverty rate decreased under Trump from 12.3 percent in 2017 to 10.5 percent in 2019. The rate of unemployment decreased from 4.4 percent to 3.7 percent, the lowest level since 1969. The number of people living in poverty decreased from 39.7 million in 2017 to 33.5 million in 2019. The inflation adjusted median household income increased from $63,467 to $64,953. Inflation itself was well under control, averaging 1.8 percent annually. Perhaps his only economic faux pas pre-COVID was increasing tariffs in 2018 (see the promises below) which reversed the beneficial aspects of the 2017 tax cuts.[12]

But then COVID hit, and all of Trump's macro numbers took a nosedive. Combining the pre- and post-Covid years, Trump's overall macro numbers were worse when he left office than when he began.

Grading a president, especially one who left office so recently, is always difficult. Given the ongoing effects of his policies, and the subjectivity involved in any assessment, it is always helpful to begin by comparing what he set out to do with what he actually did. It is typical for presidents to boast of what they will do, and Trump was certainly no exception. Let's take a look at his major objectives and compare it with the actual record.

Promise #1: Jobs, Jobs, Jobs

During his campaign Trump boasted: "I am going to be the greatest jobs president that God ever created." According to the Bureau of Labor

Statistics, in January 2017 when Trump took office there were 145,622,000 jobs, and in December 2020, his last full month in office there 142,497,000 jobs.[13] Trump was the only president in modern times to experience such a loss. While COVID is certainly to blame, the number of jobs slowed significantly in 2019, one year before COVID. This was due to his decision to raise tariffs (i.e., increasing the taxes on imports), which increased consumer prices, effectively canceling the beneficial effects of reducing tax rates a year before. The Trump tariffs invited retaliatory measures from other nations, especially China, which cumulatively increased uncertainty and reduced investment, thereby stalling jobs. By December 2020 Trump was able to recover 56 percent of the jobs lost from earlier in the year, but nevertheless, his administration still created fewer jobs during his four years than other presidents.

From 2017 to 2019 the unemployment rate steadily declined under Trump, from 4.4 percent to 3.7 percent, which was the lowest level since 3.5 percent in 1969. But then the rate skyrocketed to 8.1 percent overall in 2020, the highest level since 2012. This was due to COVID and the Trump administration's responses. In 2020 the unemployment rate peaked at 13.2 percent in April—the highest since the Great Depression—then fell to 6.7 percent in December 2020. Nevertheless, Trump left office with a higher unemployment rate than when he took office.[14]

Speaking of jobs, Trump took a particular fancy to coal miners, and the positive role that coal could play in his administration's energy policies (the USA has 25 percent of the global coal reserves), notwithstanding that coal is by far the dirtiest of the fossil fuels. While coal mining employment had slipped steadily since the 1950s due to improved technology and the movement from underground to surface mining, Trump promised to reverse this trend. Instead, there were 16.7 percent fewer coal mining jobs than when he took office.[15]

Promise #2: Significantly Reduce the Deficit and the Debt

Trump promised to significantly erase the debt and the deficit, even early on promising to erase the debt in only eight years.[16] But with the deficit situation deteriorating pre-COVID Trump made little progress. In 2016, the year before he took office, the federal budget deficit was $584.7 billion, which increased to $983 billion in 2019, largely due to the tax rate cuts. In 2020 the deficit hit $3.1 trillion, easily surpassing the previous record of $1.4 trillion in 2009. This was due to the spectacular increase in discretionary spending during his last year in office. Given the significant increases in the deficit, not surprisingly the federal debt held by the public increased from 76.2 percent in 2017 to 100.6 percent in 2020, the highest level since 1946 when it was 106.3 percent.[17]

Promise #3: Increase Economic Growth

Motivated by the tepid growth during Obama's eight years in office (the GDP growth rate never topped 2.7 percent) and especially during Obama's last year when the rate languished at 1.7 percent (the lowest since a negative growth rate of 2.6 percent in 2009). Trump promised to increase real GDP between 4 percent and 6 percent annually. He assumed that cutting taxes by itself would increase economic growth, which it did; and as a central tenet of supply-side economics, we would have expected it to. However, he basically counteracted this with a significant increase in tariffs, which effectively reduced consumer spending. Coupled with the threats of retaliatory and actual tariffs, the rate of economic growth as measured by real GDP was significantly reduced (see Figure 10.3).

Figure 10.3 Real USA GDP growth (as a percent change from the preceding period), 2016-2020

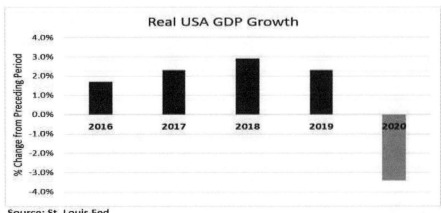

Source: St. Louis Fed

The tariffs took their toll on the economy during 2019, especially during the final two quarters when the growth of real GDP declined from 3.2 percent in the first quarter to 1.9 percent in the last. Looking at the slower GDP more closely, it was largely fueled by a sharp decrease in gross domestic private investment (i.e., business spending) from 6.4 percent in the first quarter of 2019 to a negative 6.5 percent in the last quarter of 2019.[18]

Investment in equipment decreased by 4.9 percent in the last quarter of 2019, and investment in structures (i.e., new buildings) decreased by 8.0 percent.

These numbers underscore the negative effects of tariffs on business confidence and investment. So much so that in a July–August 2019 survey of the National Association for Business Economics, 74 percent of economists expected a recession no later than 2021. Of this group, 34 percent predicted a recession by 2021; 38 percent in 2020; while 2 percent predicted a recession in 2019. As reported by *Newsweek*, some White House officials were urging a cut in the payroll tax, which did not happen.[19]

Promise #4: Reduce the Trade Deficit

This was one of Trump's goals with which I never agreed. Wealthy countries that have a booming economy typically import more than they export. They benefit from the fact that in other countries there is a lower labor cost and consequently get products at a lower price. While it is critical that we have the ability to manufacture critical products in the United States, importing from other countries has virtually raised the standard of living for nearly all Americans. It is important to realize that we import more than we export and probably always will as long as we remain the number one economy in the world.

Trump had hoped that the tariffs would increase the price of imports, thereby reducing the quantity demanded. Trump even boasted that the USA would win the war on tariffs, which shocked economists, since no one ever wins a war on tariffs, rather, both sides lose with consumers getting the short end of the stick. This is exactly what happened with the war on tariffs, and you will notice that the trade deficit did not decrease as a result of the tariffs but actually increased. Trump pledged to reduce the overall trade deficit, and especially the trade deficit with China. During Trump's four years in office the overall trade deficit increased 28 percent from $510.3 billion in 2017 to $653.9 billion in 2020. The trade deficit with China increased from $215.7 billion in 2017 to $366.1 billion in 2020, an increase of 70 percent.[20]

The Trump administration also hoped that the higher domestic prices would protect USA producers, especially in the steel and aluminum industries, resulting in more production, more jobs, and more profits. But this did not happen, largely due to retaliatory tariffs, especially from China, which increased uncertainty and reduced investment.

Promise # 5: Get Tough on Crime

In Trump's 2017 inaugural address, he promised that "the carnage of drugs, crime and poverty stops here and right now." While the poverty rate decreased from 2017 to 2019, there were 4,157 more homicides committed in 2020 than in 2016. This translates to a 2020 murder rate of 6.5 per 100,000 people, an increase of 1.1 percentage points since 2016. The 2020 rate was the highest since 1997, though still well below the peak 10.2 rate recorded in 1980. This worrisome trend has continued (and even intensified) under Biden.

In summation, Trump promised a better economic performance than Obama had delivered. Trump campaigned to increase investment, increase economic growth, reduce tax rates, reduce the federal budget deficit, reduce the trade deficit especially with China, and create jobs. Except for the reduction in tax rates, none of these promises materialized.[21]

Like most of us, I believe Trump did a lot of good things economically during his administration (the 2017 tax cuts, and that the pre-COVID economy seemed to be singing along). But the bottom line was that he spent too much money. Let's take a closer look. In 2020, the Trump administration passed five major stimulus bills, all with bipartisan support:

- The $8.3 billion Coronavirus Preparedness and Response Supplemental Appropriations Act, March 6, 2020.

- The $220 billion Families First Coronavirus Response Act, March 18, 2020.

- The $2.2 trillion CARES Act, March 27, 2020.

- The $483 billion Paycheck Protection Program and Health Care Enhancement Act, April 24, 2020.

- The $900 billion Consolidated Appropriation Act, December 28, 2020. This was a direct stimulus, but it was also passed with an end-of-year $1.4 trillion appropriations bill, which for all practical purposes was seen as one gigantic bill.

After the spring 2020 bills were passed, Mitch McConnell, at the time Senate Majority Leader, cautioned against further stimulus.[22] As 2020 progressed, the data proved him right. After peaking at 14.7 percent in April of 2020, the unemployment rate steadily decreased to 6.7 percent by November 2020. After falling 36.3 percent in the first two quarters of 2020, real GDP increased 33.8 percent in the third quarter.

These two pieces of data (along with others that were slowly trickling in) strongly evidenced that the spring stimulus programs were working and that a major stimulus-spending bill was ill advised. After all, it is well-known that macroeconomic policy takes effect with a lag. A more appropriate response would have been to wait until the first four stimulus bills had taken full effect. Or to either reduce or temporarily suspend the payroll tax (i.e., the FICA taxes on wages to fund Social Security and Medicare), which, by the way, was recommended by some of Trump's own economic advisors in 2019 as the economy took a hit from the 2018 tariffs. As the Peter G. Peterson Foundation tells us, "The payroll tax is often the primary federal tax an individual will incur. In fact, about two-thirds of households pay more in payroll taxes than income taxes."[23]

A reduction in the payroll tax would have directly put money back into the pockets of working individuals and reduced the tax burden on firms. It would have resulted in more people working, and with more people working, the budget deficit would have been reduced, resulting in fewer supply-side bottlenecks, thus reducing inflation and the need to have raised interest rates as severely as had happened.

CHAPTER 11

Americans Are Worse Off Under Biden

Not a day passes without more bad news about the economy and Biden's mismanagement. Nevertheless, in the interest of presenting a balanced assessment, I searched high and low for any good economic news. Something that would make Americans jump up and down in celebration. Anything. But no luck. I even asked my friends and my family. Oh, well.

MY TWO CENTS ON AMERICANS BEING WORSE OFF UNDER BIDEN

Reverse Biden's unacceptable decline in living standards and implement policies to ensure that this will never happen again.

So, on with bad news, of which, unfortunately, there is a plethora. Let facts be submitted to a candid world:[1]

The double whammy of inflation and unemployment, or stagflation, which has not been seen since the Jimmy Carter administration.

For anyone old enough to remember the haunting memories of stagflation during the Jimmy Carter administration, it seems like déjà vu, especially with, and not coincidentally, another inept Democratic president.

After understanding stagflation's causal factors—it is always and everywhere due to economic mismanagement—most Americans assumed that we would never live through it again, that it would be allocated to the dustbins of history. After all, stagflation "demonstrated the limits [and failure] of the postwar Keynesian consensus."[2] Right? Isn't it reasonable to assume that our leaders would never have again subjected the American people to suffer this double whammy?

But here we are, some forty odd years later, living through it. Again! Just like during the Carter years, first inflation is kicking the butts of us everyday people, and then we are hit with higher interest rates and eventually a recession, while still reeling from inflation.[3] Welcome to the worst of both worlds.

As I was writing this chapter, I received a news bulletin that we are officially in a bear market, which surprised me, since I had thought we had earned that distinction several months ago. Anyway,

> The S&P 500 is down 22 percent this year—'bear market' terrain. Between April and June [2022], households' total net worth tumbled more than $6 trillion—more than half of the $11.1 trillion in wealth that was vaporized over five quarters during the 2007- 2009 financial crisis..[4]

But hold on to your hats, there will be more stock losses (after all, this is only the second year of Biden's four-year term). Indeed,

> Market turmoil has reduced the value of pension pots (the total value of USA retirement assets fell by 4.5 percent in the first quarter) … And inflation… is cutting the purchasing power of fixed payments that those in their dotage are receiving.[5]

Cartoon 20 – Your 401K Under Biden

Rising Energy Prices

After peaking in June 2022, gasoline prices decreased by 26 percent, helping to take a notch out of the USA inflation rate.[6] But as of October 2022, gasoline prices are increasing again "threatening to inflict new pain on consumers who have been grappling with widespread inflation for more than a year."[7] This increase is attributed to the following: (1) continued tight supplies; (2) scheduled shutdowns of refineries due to maintenance and unscheduled shutdowns due to fires/accidents; (3) increase in demand for gasoline; (4) OPEC's decision to cut 2 million barrels per day.

Cartoon 21 – More 'Skyrocket' Needed Here

In addition to gasoline, other energy costs are rising, particularly the cost of electricity, which in turn has been caused by increasing natural gas prices:

Natural gas consumption is expected to set a record in 2022 as competition in the power sector from coal and nuclear has been reduced due to power plant retirements and hydroelectric output in the Western states has been reduced due to drought. Natural-gas prices have more than doubled this year because of a global supply shortage, which was exacerbated by Russia's invasion of the Ukraine, and they are expected to remain elevated for months as the fuel is needed this winter for heating and electricity generation. The tight energy supply situation in Europe is a result of its pro- 'green energy' and anti-fossil fuel policies that President Biden is trying to emulate with much apparent success. The tight supply market has increased the cost for electric utilities to purchase or generate power—costs that get passed on to customers.[8]

Natural gas prices have increased by 45 percent since July 1, 2022. Because natural gas produces 35 percent of USA electricity, it should be no surprise that in August 2022, the U.S. consumer-price index for electricity increased 15.8 percent—the biggest 12-month increase since 1981. Needless to say,

> If there is a shock to the U.S. energy system from a late-season hurricane in the Gulf of Mexico, a colder than normal winter, or an ice storm in key producing areas, natural gas and electricity prices may escalate even higher from the expected 17.2 percent increase this year.[9]

As *The Wall Street Journal* reports, one out of six US families have fallen behind on utility bills and owe a collective $16 billion, an amount that has doubled since late 2019.[10] Expect this number to keep increasing. Thanks Joe!

Stagnating Incomes

In September 2022, the Census Bureau published its annual income and poverty data on the economy. In 2021, the first year of the Biden administration, the inflation-adjusted median household income decreased slightly from that of 2020, with the difference, however, not statistically significant. Delving into the Census data a little more, several subgroups did experience statistically significant changes (at ten percent): (1) households headed by females saw their median income decline by 4.7 percent from $37,516 to $35,737; (2) Americans with some college education[11] (i.e., a high school degree but no university degree) saw their incomes decline from $67,075 to $64,378, a 4.0 percent decline; (3) Americans, 65 and older, saw their incomes decline by 2.6 percent from $48,866 to $47,620.

Persistent Inflation

Inflation has caused a lot of pain and anguish for the middle class, and for anyone on fixed incomes, especially Americans over the age of 65. This group saw their poverty rate increase from 8.9 percent in 2020 to 10.3 percent in 2021, a 16 percent increase.[12] But, as we discussed several times in this book, inflation didn't just happen. It was caused by the Biden administration and the Federal Reserve.

Rising Interest Rates

This should continue through early 2023, and perhaps beyond, reducing demand for big-ticket items, and more pain for all Americans. Given the Fed's determination to wring inflation out of our economy, a recession is just about guaranteed.

Record-Setting Debt

The federal government began fiscal year 2023 on October 1, 2022. What better Biden-way to celebrate than with a record-setting debt? Thirty-one trillion dollars to be exact. Rising interest rates will increase the debt even higher than otherwise, making the debt more costly. Biden's inflation-causing polices will add to our woes.

A daunting mess along our southern border

A record number of illegal encounters and a record number of migrant deaths, with no end in sight. As an American I am appalled by our government's exceptionally poor border performance. It has made a mockery of our insistence on law and order. Where is the law and where is the order?

Out-of-Control Homelessness

Remember our discussion of the California Gold Rush, with its genesis along the American River near Sacramento? Today, along that same river, hundreds of homeless people are camped, a stark and ironic contrast to the 1850s. While national data on homelessness from 2021-2022 is not available yet, by all accounts a significant increase is expected from the 580,000 estimated in 2020. More troubling is that in 2020 (the latest year for which such data is available), approximately six million Americans experienced severe housing cost burden in 2020, i.e., they spent more than 50 percent of their income on housing.[13] Biden's double whammy of inflation and rising interest rates will take a double toll on these Americans, as well, as of course, all of us.

Loss of confidence

What else can I say here?

The conservative social critic Victor Hanson wrote,

> If an administration deliberately wished to cause havoc on the [southern] border, to ensure fuel was nearly unaffordable, to create a crime wave, to spark 1970s hyperinflation, and to rekindle racial tensions what could it have done differently, than what President Joe Biden has done? [14]

This is not just conservative axe-grinding; even members of his own Party have expressed dissatisfaction, hopeful that someone else will be the Democratic standard bearer in 2024. With every Biden misstep this number seems to be growing.

CHAPTER 12

National Security is Paramount, Beware of China

The single most important function of a government is to provide for the national defense. To do this America must be number one in military and economic strength. In fact, it is important to realize that the number one reason the tax bill even passed was that they needed money for national defense. Currently, however, China realizes we are vastly superior militarily, so they are very cleverly using other tactics to overtake our position as the number one power.

**MY TWO-CENTS PLAN
ON NATIONAL SECURITY**

The number one objective of the US government is to provide for the national defense. Currently we have deep security concerns, and China should be our biggest fear.

China does not play by the same rules as the United States. When I went into China, a citizen of China had to have controlling interest in my company even though I supplied all the capital and technology. The amazing thing is that one day out of the blue the Chinese government came in and seized all my computers. There was no notice. They just wanted to look at all our information, and they claimed they wanted to make sure there was no conflict of interest. We did not get them back for three months. It is not uncommon for China to steal our technology. This has been going on for a long time.

An even more serious problem we face right now is that China is acquiring our farmland. In 2010 they owned 14,000 acres. As of 2020 they own 352,000 acres. It is interesting to note that Fufeng, a Chinese company, acquired 30,000 acres in North Dakota where it plans to build a wet corn milling plant. This is only twelve miles from the Grand Forks Air Force Base. According to a Fox News article, they also tried to acquire 130,000 acres near the Laughlin Air Force Base outside of Del Rio, Texas. Fortunately, we put the kibosh on that. They also tried to acquire land around Homestead Air Force Base in Florida. It is particularly important that we pay attention to the fact that they are involved in the agricultural industry. For example, they acquired Smithfield Foods, which is the largest producer of pork in the United States. In addition, they also acquired interest in the middlemen that transport it. In December of 2015, they acquired interest in Lansing Logistics, which is a company that transports food, so they have the entire infrastructure and are starting to control food products. I would pay particular attention to the Chinese trying to acquire agricultural lands in Iowa, Kansas, Michigan, and Illinois, which are strategic farming communities.

The international community takes umbrage when one nation invades another, thus vitiating their national integrity. Likewise, we cringe when we see other nations exploiting and extracting resources from a weaker nation. While this used to be the modus operandi during the nineteenth century in the age of colonialism, it no longer is, and it should no longer be tolerated.

Unfortunately, it is happening right here. The Biden administration has self-destructed the integrity of our national borders, and the administration has not only turned a blind eye, it has even encouraged the pilfering of our internal resources. To be fair, this security violation is not unique to the Biden administration, although it seems to have intensified—exacerbated by indifference and a lack of concern—under his watch.[1]

While economic causes abound, there are also political factors. A preponderant objective of any nation after securing its borders and protecting itself from external invasion (and internal anarchy) is to adequately provision for its citizens, to enable its farmers to grow enough food for its citizens. Our ability to do so is slipping away. Just look at some recent examples. Former assistant secretary of state Robert B. Charles notes that [2]

> China's overseas direct investment in "food-producing acreage" has grown tenfold in ten years. By 2020, China had amassed 35.2 million acres, 2.7 percent of US farmland. China's food-producing acreage grew an average of 2.3 million acres per year since 2015, even as China bought food producers in America's Heartland.[3]

In addition to buying US farmland, China has been hoarding food worldwide. As of mid-2022 China possesses 69 percent of global corn reserves, 60 percent of its rice and 51 percent of its wheat, while doing so has contributed to both global food insecurity and higher food prices.[4] Given China's lack of transparency, no one knows exactly how much food has been appropriated, but their role in the recent price inflation is undeniable.[5]

While outright purchase of land has raised political ire here in the USA, especially only twelve miles from Grand Forks Air Base (North Dakota), home to extremely sensitive drone technology—why was the acquisition allowed in the first place?—China has turned its attention to acquiring key assets in the global food infrastructure:

> China's agricultural involvement abroad is increasingly being done by entrenching state-owned enterprises like Cofco in the global commodity chain. By merging and acquiring agricultural businesses abroad, China is steadily gaining more control over the production process without controlling land outright.[6]

Writing in 2018, USDA economists Fred Gale and Elizabeth Gooch warned that note that more growth in investment from China appears to be forthcoming. Political leaders in China are endorsing agricultural investment as a core component of China's One Belt, One Road initiative. More investments from China in Europe and North America could offer access to agricultural technology, processing, and logistical know-how to support China's ambitions to modernize its domestic farming sector. China's goals of gaining more control over supply chains for its imports and increasing its influence on global commodity prices could drive further investment in trading, logistics, and commodity markets.[7]

It looks like this development is already underway, solidifying China's position as the number one food hoarder. But where is the outcry, the opposition to reverse these harmful policies? After all, "food is essential for survival, which is why you'd think food security would be more of a priority for our national government."[8] So why hasn't the Biden administration taken a more proactive approach?

The US House Appropriations Committee took two encouraging actions in the summer of 2022, barring companies from China (along with companies from Russia, North Korea, and Iran) from purchasing farmland and US agricultural companies. Although, as of this writing, this has not translated into national legislation directly prohibiting foreign purchases of USA food.[9] We need more thinking like New York's Republican Congresswoman Elise Stefanik, who testified "Food security is national security, and I am proud to stand up against our foreign adversaries as they attempt to exploit any potential vulnerability and assert control over our agriculture industry."[10]

A central tenet of free-market economics is that nations can trade with another on the basis of comparative advantage, and by doing so, each nation benefits from lower consumer prices, an increased array of goods, and more efficient production both domestically and globally. But at the same time, a nation should never be put in a position to worship at the altar of free trade at the expense of national security. But this is exactly what the USA is doing. In doing so, it is forfeiting any advantages of free trade by sacrificing its current and future interests. The latter comes first and foremost. Without it there is no national security. We cannot permit a situation where any nation can readily exploit the resources of another at will.

While the reasons for China's food hoarding and infrastructure buying/investing ostensibly are simple and self-explanatory,[11] there are two much deeper reasons which give cause for concern:

- A lack of international consensus and framework to stop and prevent this.

- China has been intent on replacing/usurping the global order which has been in place since the Bretton Woods conference (1944) established the IMF, World Bank, and the GATT/WTO, and elevated the USA dollar as the world's currency. China argues that it was not around during Bretton Woods, and since its national interests were excluded, it now has a right today to nudge the global order and the rules of the game to serve its interests. China is flexing its economic muscle, while sensing America's economic weakness; otherwise, it would not be so aggressive.

We must recognize that there are vital resources necessary to survive in today's world. These include lithium and uranium among others and certain inert minerals. Keep in mind that the United States only has 3 percent of the lithium in the world and China has an abundance of lithium, which is necessary for the manufacture of batteries. I believe that batteries will be a key infrastructure component much as semiconductors are today. As we move to electric vehicles, the demand will become astronomical. In short, we do not have sufficient lithium to support this; we will have to have a trade agreement with another country such as Australia and Brazil as China has a huge advantage here. We are exacerbating this advantage by allowing them to build batteries in the

United States. One of the biggest culprits is right here in Michigan where China is set to build a battery factory and the reality the State set aside $715 million in public incentives to give to them. The money is part of an exceptionally large proposal, which obscures the fact that we are setting aside $715 million to give to China to build the battery factory. This to me seems a travesty.

When it comes to essential things for our survival, the United States must control these products. Among these are steel, semiconductors, and batteries. Keep in mind that China tried to destroy our steel industry by dumping steel at below-cost levels onto the US market. Imagine trying to survive a war without the ability to manufacture steel.

One of the reasons that the United States remains so strong compared to other nations, even in a recession, is that the US dollar is the world currency. Oil is priced in US dollars; it gives us economic strength in and of itself. China has already thrown out a trial balloon that we do not need to stay with the US currency. They are attacking us on many fronts. Imagine the impact if they control more and more of the food, agricultural, and food processing industries; the semiconductor industry, which they now own; and the manufacture of batteries. We cannot acquire any land in China and yet we allow them to acquire all the land they want here—even allowing them to acquire land near a military base.

China also has secret police illegally operating in twenty-five cities around the world. We have an example of what happened in Houston. According to former US Secretary of State Michael R. Pompeo the Chinese consulate was a hub of spying and intellectual property theft. They had to close the consulate on July 23, 2020.

Regarding food and national security, my plan advocates the following policies:

- Free and fair trade amongst nations.

- Every nation has a self-determination right for its own national security, which involves the integrity of its borders, and the safeguarding of its own internal resources.

- Safeguarding our own resources that are necessary for national security and to enable our government and our economy to provide for the welfare of its citizens. To make such decisions much more transparent and based on a broad societal agreement.

- Maintain the US dollar as the global currency.

- While we should continue to trade with other countries any surpluses, after meeting domestic needs, our own food security should be prioritized. I am not suggesting that we hoard food and aggressively acquire global food producing business like China, but we need greater long-term and short-term focus on our own food security.

- A more thought-out plan to deal with China. This will be our major geopolitical challenge. Slapping tariffs on China is not the answer since tariffed nations always retaliate. China respects military might, which the USA has long had—we have the strongest military anywhere on the planet. But China also respects and defers to economic might. Here the USA has been waning, and China senses this. China as an authoritarian nation has also been flexing its muscles politically (and undemocratically) with its Intelligence Law, which encourages its citizens to spy on each other, and its establishment of police stations in foreign countries to keep tabs on its diaspora![12] Bullies never pick on the strong, only the weak and vulnerable. The best measure (both defensively and offensively) to deal with China is to get America back on track again and strengthen our economy. To make America a leader in the production of goods and services and in the production of clean energy. In addition, this is the only way to maintain the dollar as the global currency. Let us get America back on track and resuscitate its status as the premier global superpower. We need to show the world that the USA means business both figuratively and literally. Hence my America-first poilicies.

China and Global Food Prices

Name any product and chances are that China ranks at or near the top in terms of global consumption and production. As such its domestic policies will almost always affect the rest of the world's consumers and producers. A case in point: in July 2021, the Chinese government, worried about its own domestic supply of fertilizer, ordered its companies to stop exporting. At the time, China exported 24 percent of global phosphates, 13 percent of nitrogen, and 2 percent of the world's potash.[13]

Domestic prices predictably fell, while world prices increased, harming farmers worldwide. This all happened a year before the Russian invasion of Ukraine.

Another example: China, the world's largest pork consumer, consumes 48.3 percent of global production.[14] In January 2020, China reduced tariffs on pork in order to increase domestic supply and reduce prices. Then in January 2022, the government reversed policy and increased tariffs so as to benefit domestic farmers. Predictably, global prices increased. In both years global consumers and producers were at the mercy of domestic policies from China. In the USA, Iowa is our largest pork producer, accounting for one-third of USA production. Iowa is also number one in the USA for pork exports with the top five markets being Mexico, China, Japan, Canada, and South Korea. One out of every ten Iowan jobs are directly tied to pork production. So, when China abruptly decides to raise or reduce tariffs without much notice, Iowans are caught in the middle. Of course, China's ongoing food hoarding is jacking up prices worldwide adversely affecting all consumers.

So, what can we do? As I have argued elsewhere, retaliatory tariffs are self-defeating. But "what matters most is not containing China but constraining the size and suddenness of the costs that its policy choices impose on people outside its borders."[15] Obviously, this is a serious problem, and we cannot just sit idly by and ignore the fact that China has its own game plan, and its game plan is not always aligned with our best interest.

CHAPTER 13

Conclusion

L et's get America back on track with my Two-Cents plan. Here is the plan:

- Reduce the budget of every discretionary program by 2 percent and return the savings directly to the people.

- Become energy independent.

- Reduce taxes for individuals.

- Bring quality and efficiency to the federal government.

- Shrink the federal government.

- Reduce inflation to 2 percent annually.

- Simplify the tax code.

- Promote legal rather than illegal immigration.

- Re-energize the American spirit.

- Award a bonus to the managers of government bureaucracies that successfully reduce their budget.

- Put more money into the hands of American consumers and let them decide how to spend their money rather than the government.

- Recognize that our economy must be based on a sensible energy plan, rooted in our current energy availability.

- Incentivize the will to work.

- Incentivize and motivate Americans to do what we do best: innovate.

Edmund Burke, whose insights into human nature and the essence of government remain profound, wrote "Government is a contrivance of human wisdom to provide for human wants."[1] Indeed, a government should first and foremost, meet the basic wants of its citizens:

- The ability to work so that we can provide for ourselves and for our family.

- The existence (and pervasiveness) of Law and Order, without which society degenerates into anarchy.

- The protection and encouragement of private property.

- Secure national borders so that we as individuals and America as a nation can prosper.

Needless to say, the Biden administration has grossly violated this fundamental set of wants, and as Burke has warned, "history keeps a durable record of all of our acts."[2] But it is not just history that keeps a durable record of the Biden administration's economic mismanagement, it is the heart and minds of ordinary working Americans. See it in their faces. Hear it in their anguish.

Keep the American Dream Alive

When we hear about these gigantic government expenditures and deficits, let's face it, to the vast majority of us it doesn't mean anything. So the government spends another trillion or two. These numbers are so large they are meaningless. What they are really doing, however, is spending *your* money. Because we have the most industrious people in the world, our economy has always grown, and until recently we have been able to absorb the excessive government expenditures. It has only been in the last few years that they have gone completely bonkers and, in the process, have made solid efforts toward destroying the American dream.

From the time we are born we are told that one day we can go to college, buy a house, go on vacation, have a car—maybe even two cars—and one day have a family that can do the same. This has certainly been true over the years and is why people flock to America. Let's face it we have been the most upwardly mobile society in the history of all humanity. But the government is doing everything in its power to destroy that.

Let us look at what has happened as a result of government action. My office is in Troy, Michigan. In 2020 the average home, which is about 3000 square feet, sold for about $360,000.00. With 7 percent down, the monthly payment was $2,154.00. Today, two and a half years later, that same home sells for $560,000.00, and with 7 percent down, the monthly payments would be $4,160.00. My controller, who is fairly well off, bought a Grand Cherokee for $400 a month a couple years ago. That same Grand Cherokee is now $800 a month. My son goes to Michigan State University. In 1979 tuition was $29.50 per credit hour. Today, it is over $500.00 per credit hour. If it had gone up at the same rate of inflation, without government involvement, it would be under $100.00 per credit hour. When the government decided to guarantee all student loans, it opened the floodgates. Seventeen-year-olds who had no idea what it was like to have to pay back a loan could borrow unlimited amounts of money.

Obviously if we continue at this rate and don't do something about it, the American dream of owning a house and sending our kids to college will be a thing of the past for most people.

We are exceptionally optimistic by nature, and we love to be rewarded, financially and otherwise. We have always had an arrangement whereby if you provide a product or service, you receive payment for that product or service. The idea of getting riches for your efforts has motivated Americans since the beginning of the nation.

When people go to college, they generally don't get paid. In fact, on average it typically costs them in the area of $24,000-$60,000 per year just for tuition. Currently 70 percent of the people in the United States go to college and half of them end up going to grad school, law school, or medical school. On the extreme end you have a doctor who decides to go to medical school. There is four years of undergraduate school at an average of $35,551 per year and then four years of medical school at an average of $60,497 per year for a total of $384,192. Plus they had eight years of not getting paid for working a job. If they made $40,000 per year, $14,132 less than the median income for the United States, the opportunity costs would be the $320,000 they did not earn. They are sacrificing because of the dream. In the end the medical school really cost them $700,000 plus probably having to work twice as hard as they would had they had a job.

To say that we are optimistic may be the understatement of the century. More than 16 percent of people in the United States become entrepreneurs. They all know that four out of five businesses fail within the first five years, but that does not stop them because they are positive they are going to be the ones that succeed. When they start these companies, they are putting in sixty-, seventy-, even eighty-hour weeks. Not only are they not making minimum wage, they are generally losing money for one, maybe two or even three years or longer, but that does not stop them. In fact, they are excited because they have that dream. They know that one day they will make it. We may be the biggest risk takers in the world, but we have always believed in ourselves because we know that in the end we will succeed.

Let's face it this country is made up of dreamers and has been made up of dreamers since its inception. When the Pilgrims came over, they had a dream of religious freedom. When the colonists were here, many of their dreams at the time seemed so unrealistic that they were absurd. We had a handful of people who had no guns, no training, and a fledgling general by the name of George Washington who had to fight the most powerful army on the planet. But in the end, they overcame all adversity to form a unique country with a unique set of values. A nation founded on the principles of life, liberty, and the pursuit of happiness. But above all we had a characteristic inherent in virtually everyone that was probably the most powerful force impacting America's great success. We were the most optimistic people on Earth. Our forefathers pioneered in so many areas. We had Vanderbilt and the railroads, Rockefeller and oil, Carnegie and steel, Thomas Edison and his inventions, and Henry Ford with the automobile. We continue to lead the charge in the areas of computers and IT, the internet and artificial intelligence, and even the electric car.

For decades we have also championed the opportunity for the little guy. Now, the government is trying to squash that effort. When the government spends a trillion dollars, that is $6,200 per tax filer. It does not hurt the billionaires but does squeeze the average American. We know that for about twenty years we have had about a 2 percent rate of inflation per year until the government decided to go hog wild with its spending. When it threw all that money into the economy when no additional goods or services were provided, we obviously caused idiotic inflation induced by the government. So, when you go to the store and spend over 100 percent more for eggs or milk, you can thank the government. When you go to the gas station and spend 50 percent more for gas than you should, you can thank the government. When you try to buy a house and find that your monthly payments are 100 percent higher than they were two and a half years ago, again, you can thank the government. When your son or daughter wants to go to college and the tuition is five times what it should be, again, you can thank the government.

Americans have always been able to overcome adversity. This time it is no different. I am confident we will persevere and extricate ourselves from the damage done by the government. My Two-Cent plan will solve the problem. Certainly, it is time to put the government on a diet. We are a nation that has incredible resources, but the greatest resource is our people. We have a fire inside us that is a beacon that drives us. Our unbridled optimism that we share is an enormous asset. Let us take advantage of all these strengths and keep that American Dream alive!

Notes

Chapter 2: Taming Inflation

[1] Steve Boggan, *Gold Fever: One Man's Adventures on the Trail of the Gold Rush* (New York: Simon & Schuster, 2015).

[2] Boggan, *Gold Fever*.

[3] N. Gregory Mankiw, *Principles of Economics*, 9th ed. (Boston: Cengage, 2021), 630.

[4] See Friedrich A. Hayek, "The Use of Knowledge in Society," *The American Economic Review*, Vol. 35, No. 4, 1945, 519-530, for an eloquent discussion of the beneficent workings of relative prices.

[5] Mankiw, Principles of Economics, 630.

[6] Jack Nicas and Ana Lankes, "Think 9% percent Inflation is Bad? Try 90% per-cent," *New York Times*, August 6, 2022, https://www.nytimes.com/2022/08/06/business/inflation-argentina.html?searchResultPosition=4

[7] Martin Feldstein, "Argentina and Inflation: What the rest of the world can learn," World Economic Forum, January 3, 2017, https://www.weforum.org/agenda/2017/01/argentina-and-inflation-what-the-rest-of-the-world-can-learn.

[8] See "Throughout history," *The Economist,* March 12, 2020; and Jorda et al., 2020.

[9] "Keeping the Lights on: How to Stop Europe's energy crunch from spiraling into an economic crisis," *The Economist,* September 3, 2022, 65.

[10] Although created by an act of Congress (i.e., the 1913 Federal Reserve Act) under the auspices of Article I, Section VIII of the US Constitution, the Federal Reserve is not technically part of the government. It conducts its own monetary policies, not subject directly to the will of the voters. Congress can, however, modify, amend, or even abolish the 1913 Act if it chooses.

[11] Specifically, M1 includes currency in circulation, checkable bank deposits, and savings deposits. M2 includes M1, small time deposits (less than $100,000) and money market funds. Since M2 includes M1, the former is larger than the latter. See "Money Stock Measures-H.6 Release," The Federal Reserve, September 27, 2022, https://www.federalreserve.gov/releases/h6/Current/.. Note: In May of 2020, the Fed revised its money supply definitions by moving savings deposits from M2 to M1.

[12] Francesco Bianchi and Leonardo Melosi, "Inflation as a Fiscal Limit," Federal Re-serve Bank of Chicago, August 29, 2022, Working paper 2022-37, 3, https://doi.org/10.21033/wp-2022-37.

[13] A non-government agency, The National Bureau of Economic Research, officially decides when a recession begins and when it ends. Needless to say, the official ending date does not usually coincide with the unofficial effects on ordinary Americans.

[14] "After the pandemic, will inflation return?" The Economist, December 12, 2020, https://www.economist.com/leaders/2020/12/12/after-the-pandemic-will-inflation-return.

---

[15] John Greenwood and Steve H. Hanke, "Too Much Money Portends High Inflation: The Fed Should Pay Attention to Milton Friedman's Wisdom," *The Daily Hatch*, July 20, 2021, https://thedailyhatch.org/2021/08/08/the-fed-should-pay-attention-to-milton-friedmans-wisdom/.

[16] Irina Ivanova, "Buckle up, America: The Fed wants to put you out of a job," CBS News, September 30, 2022, https://www.msn.com/en-us/money/markets/buckle-up-america-the-fed-wants-to-put-you-out-of-a-job/ar-AA12aKU7.

[17] You would think that at the very least we would elect the Fed's Board of Governors (headed by Jerome Powell) and the Federal Open Market Committee (responsible for conducting monetary policy on a daily basis). But not so. They are all appointed and not elected.

[18] Art Laffer, interviewed in 2019, said, "The Fed shouldn't be independent of the administration. Never should be. None of those people were elected. They were appointed" ([Nikki Schwab, "Laffer: Federal Reserve shouldn't be independent from White House," *New York Post*, June 30, 2019, https://nypost.com/2019/06/30/laffer-federal-reserve-shouldnt-be-independent-from-white-house/.) In the same interview he recommended Friedman's interesting essay "Should There Be an independent Monetary Authority" (Freidman, 1962) reprinted *In Search of a Monetary Constitution* (Yeager, 1962). It is well worth a read.

[19] This is the Fed's main interest rate, and the only rate that it directly controls. As the federal funds rate increases, so do other interest rates, including the prime rate, which banks usually reserve for the best customers.

[20] Ivanova, "Buckle up, America.

[21] Ivanova, "Buckle up, America."

[22] The Federal Open Market Committee (FMOC) implements monetary policy. It is comprised of the seven members of the Fed's Board of Governors (that is, when there are seven members) and five of the presidents of the Fed's Twelve district banks, appointed on a rotating basis, e.g., the Federal Reserve Bank of Richmond, the Federal Reserve Bank of Dallas, etc. Incidentally, no one on the FOMC or the Board of Governors is directly elected by the people.

[23] Collin Eaton and Jennifer Hiller, "As Gasoline Prices Drop, Electricity and Some Heating Costs Rise," The Wall Street Journal, September 13, 2022, https://www.wsj.com/articles/as-gasoline-prices-drop-electricity-and-some-heating-costs-rise-11663096992?page=1.

[24] This data was obtained from the Federal Reserve Bank of St. Louis.

[25] "Central bankers worry that a new era of high inflation is beginning," *The Economist*, September 3, 2022, https://www.economist.com/finance-and-economics/2022/08/30/central-bankers-worry-that-a-new-era-of-high-inflation-is-beginning?utm_medium=cpc.adword.pd&utm_source=google&ppccampaignID=17210591673&ppcadID=&utm_campaign=a.22brand_pmax&utm_content=conversion.direct-response.anony-mous&gclid=Cj0KCQiAxbefBhDfARIsAL4XLRrYE0s2Ms1-bTJO87OvhqNp_v5P9gaXHMbGm6TUoZuOxNBr3cQFjf-gaAhHhEALw_wcB&gclsrc=aw.ds.

[26] Friedman (1912-2006) was (and is, given that his influence is still pervasive) one of the most influential economists. A free-market conservative, he was best known for his work on monetarism and the consumption function (i.e., how, and why we consume). He taught at the University of Chicago, where he helped develop the Chicago School, which was influential in rejecting the then- dominant, government-laden Keynesian economics. He advised both Margaret Thatcher and Ronald Reagan. After retiring from the University of Chicago, he became a resident scholar at the Hoover Institute. He was awarded the Nobel Prize in economics in 1976. One of my favorite books, and highly recommended for all Americans, is *Capitalism and Freedom* (1962) in which he adeptly argues that we should rely less on government and more on the market.

27 Ivan Illan, "Money Velocity Iis at an All-Time Low: Why does it Matter?" *Forbes*, April 25, 2022, https://www.forbes.com/sites/forbesfinancecouncil/2022/04/25/money-velocity-is-at-an-all-time-low-why-does-it-matter/?sh=50acc7d83dfa.

28 Mankiw, *Principles of Economics*, 621.

29 Greenwood and Hanke, "Too Much Money Portends High Inflation."

30 "The Inflation Acceleration Action," The Economist, August 27, 2022, https://www.economist.com/leaders/2022/08/08/americas-climate-plus-spending-bill-is-flawed-but-essential.

31 Alex Durate and William McBride, "Reminder that Corporate Taxes are the Most Economically Damaging Way to Increase Revenue," American Tax Foundation, August 12, 2022, https://taxfoundation.org/inflation-reduction-act-corporate-taxes/.

32 "America's climate-plus spending bill is flawed but essential," The Economist, August 8, 2022, https://www.economist.com/leaders/2022/08/08/americas-climate-plus-spending-bill-is-flawed-but-essential.

33 Richard Rubin and Theo Francis, "Amazon, Berkshire Hathaway Could Be Among Top Payers of New Minimum Tax," *Wall Street Journal*, September 25, 2022, https://www.wsj.com/articles/amazon-berkshire-hathaway-could-be-among-top-payers-of-new-minimum-tax-11664098382?page=1.

34 "Growing the IRS ill-advised," Editorial, *Orange County Register*, August 18, 2022, https://www.ocregister.com/2022/08/16/growing-the-irs-growing-government/

35 Excluded are stocks contributed to retirement accounts, pensions, and ESOPS.

36 Exempt from the tax, however, are the smallest producers, who produce less than the CO_2 equivalent of 25,000 tons/year. These small producers, however, account for 60 percent of total US energy methane emissions.

37 Myles McCormick, "Oil industry condemns first US fee on greenhouse gases amid energy crisis," Financial Times, September 3, 2022, https://www.ft.com/content/b6fd6ac1-8715-4d0d-b45c-ddb161ebf621.

38 Durate and McBride, "Reminder that Corporate Taxes are the Most Economically Damaging Way to Increase Revenue."

39 Durate and McBride, "Reminder that Corporate Taxes are the Most Economically Damaging Way to Increase Revenue."

40 Rothman, Lily, "Putting the Rising Cost of College in Perspective," Time, August 31, 2016, https://time.com/4472261/college-cost-history/.

41 Fees and tuition are usually reported together. Tuition, of course is the money collected for direct instruction, whereas, fees are wide ranging, including student government, transportation, laboratories, athletic facilities, the library, etc. Needless to say, student fees differ widely between campuses.

42 *National Center for Education Statistics*, 2022, Table 316.10. This is more or less in the same ballpark for the data for all four-year colleges and universities, both public and private: a four-fold increase in the cost of tuition and fees after controlling for inflation. For two-year colleges, tuition and fees increased three-fold during the same period, after controlling for inflation, while room and board increased two-fold. So, it seems, just from this superficial analysis, that the crux of the problem is especially with private, non-profit four-year colleges and universities.

43 University of Massachusetts, Amherst 2022; and Hewitt (1988). The data listed are in current dollars.

[44] "Income, Poverty and Health Insurance Coverage in the United States: 2021," US Census Bureau, September 13, 2022, https://www.census.gov/newsroom/press-releases/2022/income-poverty-health-insurance-coverage.html.

[45] The source for the current median income is The United States Census Bureau, December 28, 1967, Income in 1966 of Families and Persons in the United States, Report P60-53.

[46] Lyss Welding, "Student Loan Debt by Year," BestColleges.com, October 3, 2022, https://www.bestcolleges.com/research/student-loan-debt-by-year/.

[47] Philip Yeagle, "The High Cost of College Athletics and Your Tuition, *HuffPost*, June 4, 2015, https://www.huffpost.com/entry/may-you-get-what-you-pay_b_7503068.

[48] Adam Smith, *An Inquiry into the Nature and Causes of the Wealth of Nations*, Vol. II, Bk. V, Pt. 3, Article 2, (Chicago: University of Chicago Press, 1976), 284; originally published by W. Strahan and T. Cadell, London, 1776.

[49] Shannon Chamberlin, "The Radical, 18th Century Scottish System for Paying for College," *The Atlantic*, February 2, 2016, https://www.theatlantic.com/business/archive/2016/02/college-cost-18th-century-scotland/459387/.

[50] The data in this paragraph was obtained from 'Current-fund expenditures of institutions of higher education, by purpose: 1980-81 to 1992-93 (1996); Digest of Education Statistics, "Total expenditures of private nonprofit degree-granting postsecondary institutions," National Center for Education Statistics, https://nces.ed.gov/programs/digest/d16/tables/dt16_334.40.asp..

[51] Digest of Education Statistics, "Total expenditures of private nonprofit degree-granting postsecondary institutions," National Center for Education Statistics, https://nces.ed.gov/programs/digest/d16/tables/dt16_334.40.asp. Academic support includes activities and services that support the institution's primary mission of instruction, research, and public service. Student services includes intercollegiate athletics and student health services except when they operate as self-supporting auxiliary enterprises. These can include food services, residence halls, and athletic teams. Hospital services includes fees connected with hospitals directly connected with the college/university..

[52] Anqi Chen, Alicia H. Munnell, Geoffrey T. Sanzenbacher, and Alice Zulkarnain, "Why Has U.S. Life Expectancy Fallen Below Other Countries?" Center for Retirement Research at Boston College, December 2017, Number 17-22, https://crr.bc.edu/wp-content/uploads/2017/11/IB_17-22.pdf.

[53] "Our global reach," Organisation for Economic Co-operation and Development, https://www.oecd.org/about/members-and- partners/#:~:text=Today percent2C percent20our percent2038 percent20Member percent20countries,out percent20in percent20the percent20OECD percent20Convention.

[54] Matthew McGough, Imani Telesford, Shameek Rakshit, Emma Wager, Krutika Amin, and Cynthia Cox, "How does health spending in the U.S. compare to other countries?" Peterson KFF Health System Tracker, February 9, 2023, https://www.healthsystemtracker.org/chart-collection/health-spending-u-s-compare-countries-2/#GDP%20per%20capita%20and%20health%20consumption%20spending%20per%20capita,%202020%20(U.S.%20dollars,%20.

[55] Francesco Bianchi and Leonardo Melosi, "Inflation as a Fiscal Limit," Federal Re-serve Bank of Chicago, August 29, 2022, Working paper 2022-37, 3-4, https://doi.org/10.21033/wp-2022-37.

[56] "Consumer Prices in America: The Perils of Wishful Thinking, Editorial," *The Economist*, September 17, 2022, 11, 65.

[57] Despite the visible effects of food and energy (our basic needs) on the budget of ordinary Americans, the Fed prefers the core inflation rate, for tracking long-term consumer spending and incomes. The core rate tracks goods (both durable and non-durable) and services typically bought by consumers, such as health care and housing. However, higher energy

prices by increasing transportation costs increases the prices of a wide array of consumer goods and services.

58 "Consumer Prices in America."

59 The FOMC, the Fed's main policy implementing arm, will be meeting on November 1-2 and December 13-14, 2022, and then on January 31-February 1, 2023, with almost monthly meetings thereafter. It is a good bet that the FOMC will increase the federal funds rate in both of its 2022 meetings, and in its Jan/Feb 2023 meeting as well.

Chapter 3: Incentivizing America's Workers

1 Compared to the G-7 nations (the group of seven richest nations), only Canada and Italy have a lower labor force participation rate than the US.

2 In 1948, the labor force participation rate of prime-aged women was 30 percent. It continually increased (due to changing culture values enabling and encouraging more women to work) peaking at 76.8 percent in 1998, which, by the way, was more than enough to offset the continuous decline of prime-aged men. The percentage of prime-aged women dropping out of the labor force to care for children, and/or a sick relative is currently 60 percent, trending down from 80 percent in 1990. This downward trend reflects that today, more educated women are delaying childbirth. (Data obtained from the Bureau of Labor Statistics.)

3 In an interesting study by Jaroszewicz et al. (2022) found that people who received a small amount of cash during the pandemic (tantamount to a stimulus check) reported worse financial, psychological, and health outcomes and became more unhappy post-stimulus by teasing them into what they cannot afford. (Jaroszewicz, Ania and Jachimowicz, Jon and Hauser, Oliver and Jamison, Julian, How Effective Is (More) Money? Randomizing Unconditional Cash Transfer Amounts in the US (July 5, 2022). Available at SSRN: https://ssrn.com/abstract=4154000 or http://dx.doi.org/10.2139/ssrn.4154000.)

4 Terry Jones, "Labor Force Participation Rate Mystery: Why Have So Many Americans Stopped Working?", *Investor's Business Daily*, February 14, 2020, https://www.investors.com/news/labor-force-participation-rate-low/.

5 Didem Tüzemen, "Why Are Prime-Age Men Vanishing from the Labor Force?" Federal Reserve Bank of Kansas City, February 21, 2018, https://www.kansascityfed.org/research/economic-review/1q18-tuzemen-why-prime-age-men-vanishing/.

6 Officially known as "An Act to Establish a Clear and Comprehensive Prohibition of Discrimination on the Basis of Disability."

7 These objectives were strengthened and clarified with the ADA amendments of 2008.

8 For a good discussion on the intricacies of the ADA, see Thomas C. Weiss, "The ADA and Employee Leave Protections," *Disabled World*, September 17, 2012, www.disabledworld.com/disability/discrimination/ada/employee- leave.php.

9 Terry Jones, "Labor Force Participation Rate Mystery."

10 Medicare and Social Security will be discussed in Chapter 6.

11 Rachel Garfield, Robin Rudowitz, and Anthony Damico, "Understanding the Intersection of Medicaid and Work," Henry J. Kaiser Family Foundation, January 2018, https://files.kff.org/attachment/Issue-Brief-Understanding-the-Intersection-of-Medicaid-and-Work.

12 Krueger Alan B., "Where Have All the Workers Gone? An Inquiry into the Decline of the U.S. Labor Force Participation Rate," Brookings Institution, September 7-8, 2017, BPEA Conference Drafts, https://www.brookings.edu/bpea-articles/where-have-all-the-workers-gone-an-inquiry-into-the-decline-of-the-u-s-labor-force-participation-rate/

[13] Krueger, "Where Have All the Workers Gone?

[14] For a brief history of opioid use see *The History of Opioids in the US*, 2016.

[15] The study notes that "Approximately 77 million Americans, or 1 in 3 adults, have a criminal record. Having a criminal record can make it difficult, or even impossible, for an individual to work in a given field."

[16] Jennifer Doleac, "Can Employment-Focused Programs Reduce Reincarceration Rates?" Econfact, June 29, 2018, https://econofact.org/can-employment-focused-reentry-programs-keep-former-prisoners-from-being-reincarcerated.

[17] A study of 1.7 million formerly incarcerated individuals released from the California prison system between 1993 and 2008, found that construction and manufacturing opportunities, at the time of This is not a perfect solution (no solution can ever be), but it is a necessary first step. It kills two birds with one stone: first it rehabilitates individuals who have paid their debt to society and second it increases the LFPR. This is not to say that every employer should go out of their way to hire a formerly incarcerated individual but let's not automatically exclude them as a possible candidate release, were associated with significant reductions in recidivism, whereas the availability of low wage jobs had no significant effect (Schnepel 2018).

[18] Elizabeth Arias, Betzaida Tejada-Vera, Kenneth D. Kochanek, and Farida B. Ahmad, "Life Expectancy Estimates for 2021," U.S. Department of Health and Human Services, Centers for Disease Control and Prevention, National Center for Health Statistics, August 2022, https://www.cdc.gov/nchs/products/index.htm.

[19] Christopher Farell, "Working Longer May Benefit Your Health," *New York Times*, March 3, 2017, https://www.nytimes.com/2017/03/03/business/retirement/working-longer-may-benefit-your-health.html.

[20] "Twenty-Five Health benefits of Enjoying Your Job," Dr. HealthBenefits.com 2022, https://drhealthbenefits.com.

[21] Farell, "Working Longer May Benefit Your Health."

[22] Kim Parker, "What's behind the growing gap between men and women in college completion?," November 8, 2021, https://www.pewresearch.org/fact-tank/2021/11/08/whats-behind-the-growing-gap-between-men-and-women-in-college-completion/

[23] Erin Duffin, "Undergraduate enrollment in the U.S. 1970-2030, by gender," May 18, 2022, https://www.statista.com/statistics/236360/undergraduate-enrollment-in-us-by-gender/.

[24] Elka Torpey, "Education pays," Bureau of Labor Statistics, June 2021, https://www.bls.gov/careeroutlook/2021/data-on-display/education-pays.htm

[25] Lochner, Lance, "Nonproduction Benefits of Education: Crime, Health, and Good Citizenship," in Eric A. Hanushek, Stephen Manchin, and Ludger Woessman (Eds.) Handbook of the Economics of Education, Volume 4, Elsevier, Amsterdam, 2011, 183-282.

[26] Ryan Farrell and William Lawhorn, "Fast-growing occupations that pay well and don't require a college degree," Monthly Labor Review, June 2022, https://www.bls.gov/careeroutlook/2022/article/occupations-that-dont-require-a-degree.htm.

Chapter 4: Becoming Energy Independent

[1] Rhodes, Richard, *Energy: A Human History* (New York: Simon and Schuster, 2018).

[2] Brigham McCown, "Tackling Inflation Requires Energy Clarity," Real Clear Energy, September 21, 2022, https://www.realclearenergy.org/articles/2022/09/21/tackling_inflation_requires_energy_clarity_854635.html.

[3] "World Nuclear Power Reactors & Uranium Requirements," World Nuclear Associ-ation, September 2022, https://www.world-nuclear.org/information-library/facts-and-fig-ures/world-nuclear-power-reactors-and-uranium-requireme.aspx. Compare this to the world's leader, France which obtains 69 percent of its electricity from nuclear energy, and Belgium 50.8 percent. Interestingly China's nuclear energy provides only 5 percent of its electricity, while relying on coal for 69 percent, a situation similar to the USA about fifty years ago.

[4] Timothy Puko and Anthony DeBarros, "Federal Leases Slow to a Trickle Under Biden," *Wall Street Journal*, September 4, 2022, https://www.wsj.com/articles/federal-oil-leases-slow-to-a-trickle-under-biden-11662230816.

[5] Puko and DeBarros, "Federal Leases Slow to a Trickle Under Biden."

[6] Timothy Puko, "Biden Administration Awards Offshore Oil-and-Gas Leases for 1.7 Million Acres in Gulf of Mexico," Wall Street Journal, September 14, 2022, https://www.wsj.com/articles/biden-administration-awards-offshore-oil-and-gas-leases-for-1-7-million-acres-in-gulf-of-mexico-11663192635. These two presidents have the dis-tinction of issuing the fewest number of leases since 1960.

[7] For interesting and encouraging examples, see Rhodes's *Energy: A Human History* (2018), Freece (2003), and Yergin (1991).

[8] "New Technology makes it possible to monitor, manage, and minimize methane leaks," *The Economist*, June 23, 2022, https://www.economist.com/technology-quar-terly/2022/06/23/new-technology-can-help-monitor-manage-and-minimise-methane-leaks.

[9] "New Technology makes it possible to monitor, manage, and minimize methane leaks."

[10] Rounding out the top five: France with 56 reactors at 13 percent of the global total, China (54 and 12.4 percent), Russia (37 and 8.5 percent), and Japan (33 and 7.6 percent).

[11] "World Nuclear Performance Report 2022," World Nuclear Association, July 2022, https://www.world-nuclear.org/getmedia/9dafaf70-20c2-4c3f-ab80-f5024883d9da/World-Nuclear-Performance-Report-2022.pdf.aspx.

[12] Most of our uranium is mined in the Colorado Plateau, stretching over Arizona, New Mex-ico, Utah, and Colorado.

[13] "Energy security gives climate-friendly nuclear power plants a new appeal," *The Economist*, June 25, 2022, https://www.economist.com/briefing/2022/06/23/energy-security-gives-climate-friendly-nuclear-power-plants-a-new-appeal.

[14] Rhodes, *Energy: A Human History*, 230.

[15] Rhodes, *Energy: A Human History*, 231-34

[16] Megan Lampinen, "Are Electric Vehicle Projections Underestimating Demand?", Automo-tive World, March 30, 2021, https://www.automotiveworld.com/articles/are-electric-ve-hicle-projections-underestimating-demand/.

[17] Melissa Pistilli, "Lithium Investing: 8 Top Lithium Producing Countries," Investing News, September 8, 2022, https://investingnews.com/daily/resource-investing/battery-metals-investing/lithium-investing/lithium-production-by-country/.

[18] Niclas Rolander, Jesper Starn, and Elisabeth Behrmann, "Lithium Batteries' Dirty Secret: Manufacturing Them Leaves Massive Carbon Footprint," Industry Week, Oc-tober 16, 2018, https://www.industryweek.com/technology-and-iiot/article/22026518/lithium-bat-teries-dirty-secret-manufacturing-them-leaves-massive-carbon-footprint.

[19] Given the necessity of heating the raw lithium ore to 2000 degrees Fahrenheit, fossil fuels are needed, at least right now, and renewable energy is not a viable option in the produc-tion, mining, or preparation stages.

[20] In 2021, the largest producers were Australia, 52 percent; Chile, 24.7 percent; and China 13.3 percent (Pistilli, "Lithium Investing: 8 Top Lithium Producing Countries"). Note: the USA produces its lithium from one mine in Nevada and withholds its production totals for proprietary purposes. Perusing several sources seems to indicate that the USA produces 1 percent of global lithium production.

[21] Chile and Australia possess approximately two-thirds of global lithium reserves, while China has 6.8 percent of global reserves. ('Reserves of Lithium Worldwide as of 2021,' by Country, Statista, 2022). Since 2016, global reserves of lithium have increased from 14 million metric tons to 22 million metric tons, an increase of 57 percent. Look for near-term supply to increase, but not as much as demand (Fildes, 2022). This will cause the price of Lithium to rise, thus making more reserves economically viable.

[22] Ethanol figures are obtained from the Energy Information Administration August 8, 2022.

[23] The USA ranks 9th at 4.0 percent, and Russia ranks 6th, at 6.2 percent

[24] "Split Reality: Sanctions have been less effective than hoped," *The Economist*, August 27, 2022, 56.

[25] "Keeping the Lights on: How to Stop Europe's energy crunch from spiraling into an economic crisis," *The Economist,* September 3, 2022.

[26] At this point it is not clear which nations will go along with this; perhaps all of the G-7 nations but India and China, which are major consumers of Russian fossil fuels.

Chapter 5: Fixing the Border

[1] Migrants can either emigrate or immigrate. To emigrate means to leave one's native country, and to immigrate means to enter a non-native country. While gray areas exist between the two, overall, a migrant is temporarily moving from one country to another without a permanent home, whereas an immigrant intends a permanent change of residency. A border encounter is either an apprehension in which a migrant is taken into custody in the USA to await adjudication, or an expulsion, in which a migrant is immediately expelled to his/her home country or last country of transit without being held in U.S. custody. Since Biden took office, the percentage of migrants expelled has greatly decreased from 93 percent in May 2020, to 47 percent in July 2021 (John Gramlich, "Migrant encounters at U.S. Mexico border are at a 21-year high," Pew Research Center, August 13, 2021).

[2] John Gramlich and Alissa Scheller, "What's Happening at the US Mexico Border in 7 Charts," Pew Research Center, November 9, 2021, https://www.pewresearch.org/fact-tank/2021/11/09/whats-happening-at-the-u-s-mexico-border-in-7-charts/.

[3] Gramlich, "Migrant encounters at U.S. Mexico border are at a 21-year high."

[4] There has been a strong, recent upsurge in immigrants from the Northern Triangle due to violence, crime, and corruption. See the analysis by the Pew Research Center (2017).

[5] Camilo Montoya-Galvez, "U.S. Annual U.S. border arrivals top 2 million, fueled by record migration from Venezuela, Cuba and Nicaragua," CBS News, September 20, 2022, https://www.cbsnews.com/news/annual-u-s-border-arrests-top-2-million-fueled-by-record-migration-from-venezuela-cuba-and-nicaragua/.

[6] Gramlich and Scheller, "What's Happening at the US Mexico Border in 7 Charts."

[7] In April 2022, President Biden tried to lift Title 42, but given the ensuing controversy, particularly over whether this was best time to lift it and whether it is too soon, it has remained in place.

[8] Katherine Fung, "Is the Border More Secure Under Biden than Trump? What we Know," Newsweek, September 16, 2022, https://www.newsweek.com/us-southern-border-more-secure-joe-biden-donald-trump-1743839.

[9] Federation of American Immigration Reform (FAIR), "FAIR Analysis: 4.9 Million Illegal Aliens Have Crossed our Borders Since President Biden Took Office," August 16, 2022, https://www.fairus.org/press-releases/border-security/fair-analysis-49-million-illegal-aliens-have-crossed-our-borders.

[10] "FAIR Reveals that Illegal Aliens Released into the U.S. Under Biden Will Cost American Taxpayers an Additional $20.4 Billion Annually," September 13, 2022, https://www.fairus.org/press-releases/presidential-administration/workforce-economy/fair-reveals-illegal-aliens-released.

[11] "FAIR Reveals that Illegal Aliens Released into the U.S. Under Biden Will Cost American Taxpayers."

[12] "New FAIR Cost Study: Biden Immigration Policies Impose Crushing Burden on Already-Strained Schools," September 16, 2022, https://www.fairus.org/press-releases/publications-resources/new-fair-cost-study-biden-immigration-policies-impose.

[13] Cadena, Brian, Brain Duncan, and Stephen J. Trejo, "The Labor Market Integration and Impacts of US Immigrants," in Barry R. Chiswick and Paul W. Miller (eds.) *Handbook of the Economics of International Migration*, Elsevier Press, Amsterdam, 1197-1259. Card, David, "Is New Immigration Really So Bad?" *Economic Journal*, Vol. 115, Issue 506, November 2005, pp. 1337-1357.

[14] Jon Baselice, Immigration Data Center, U.S. Chamber of Commerce, 2022, https://www.uschamber.com/immigration/immigration-data-center.

[15] "America's legal-immigration system remains gummed up," The Economist, July 28, 2022, https://www.economist.com/united-states/2022/07/28/americas-legal-immigration-system-remains-gummed-up.

[16] Priscilla Alvarez, "More Cubans are coming to the US by sea than any time since the 1990s," CNN, September 23, 2022, https://www.cnn.com/2022/09/23/politics/immigration-cuba-haiti-ocean-coast-guard/index.html.

[17] Maria Venacio, Karla Nordarse, and Oliver Isabella, "Cuban Migration is Changing, the US Must Take Note," WOLA: Advocacy for Human Rights in the Americas, March 25, 2022, https://www.wola.org/analysis/cuban-migration-is-changing-us-must-note/ (emphasis added).

[18] Statistics were obtained from Pew Research Center (September 2019).

Chapter 6: Rescuing Social Security and Medicare

[1] "Payroll Taxes: What are they and what do they fund?" Peter G. Peterson Foundation, April 8, 2021, https://www.pgpf.org/budget-basics/budget-explainer-payroll-taxes.

[2] Anne Tergesen, "Inflation Pushes Social Security COLA to 8.7% percent in 2023, Highest Increase in Four Decades," The Wall Street Journal, October 13, 2022, https://www.wsj.com/articles/social-security-benefits-to-increase-in-2023-11665665206. Social Security COLAs began in 1975. The record increase was 14.3 percent in 1980.

[3] Tergesen, "Inflation Pushes Social Security COLA to 8.7% percent in 2023, Highest Increase in Four Decades."

[4] Trevor Jennewine, "2023 Will Bring 3 Big Changes to Social Security: Here's What Retirees Must Know," The Motley Fool, September 17, 2022, https://www.msn.com/en-us/money/retirement/2023-will-bring-3-big-changes-to-social-security-here-s-what-retirees-must-know/ar-AA11XNqB?ocid=msedgntp&cvid=80e018a47dbf4f1190ab3194b520afed.

[5] Only 24 **percent** of USA workers are covered by a pension. Eighty-one percent of today's retirees receive some income from a pension plan, and for 42 percent of these people, their

pension provides half or more of their retirement income, according to a study by the Insured Retirement Institute (IRI).

Chapter 7: Reducing the Deficit and Debt

[1] While the string of budget surpluses from 1920-1930 was nothing to sneeze at.

[2] John Steele Gordon, *Hamilton's Blessing: The Extraordinary Life and Times of Our National Debt* (New York: Penguin Books, 1998).

[3] The 2022 Long-Term Budget Outlook, Congressional Budget Office, July 2022, https://www.cbo.gov/system/files/2022-07/57971-LTBO.pdf.

[4] When the federal government runs a deficit, it is the US Treasury's job to raise the requisite funds. The debt is defined as the sum of outstanding loans that the US Treasury has borrowed from individuals and institutions, both domestic and foreign, to finance annual budget deficits.

[5] Mr. Jackson was also quite stingy in infrastructure spending. Jackson, by the way, refused to renew the charter of the Second Bank of the United States (the USA's central bank at the time), which contributed to the Panic.

[6] When discussing the debt, two measures are used: (1) total federal debt, which includes intra- government borrowing/lending, e.g., the Social Security Administration often borrows from the US Treasury; and (2) the debt held by the public, which excludes intragovernment lending. In this chapter, unless otherwise stated, we will use the debt held by the public, since it better indicates an administration's macro effects.

[7] "Why Should We Worry about the National Debt?" Committee for a Responsible Federal Budget, April 16, 2019, https://www.crfb.org/papers/why-should-we-worry-about-national-debt.

[8] "Why Should We Worry about the National Debt?"

[9] The Committee warns that if the debt increases too high, or the federal government loses its commitment to fight inflation, interest rates could rise even faster as investors demand protection or hastily sell off their bonds.

[10] "Why Should We Worry about the National Debt?"

[11] "Why Should We Worry about the National Debt?"

[12] As long as budget deficits are above zero, then the federal debt will increase, even if the budget deficit is decreasing. Thus, the only way to reduce the debt and to sustainably reduce interest payments is to run budget surpluses.

Chapter 8: Reducing Discretionary Spending

[1] These figures are nominal, meaning they are measured in the actual prices of the time.

[2] The figures in these two paragraphs are taken from the Congressional Budget Office (2022).

[3] Smith, *Wealth of Nations*), Vol. II, Bk. IV, Ch. 1, Pt 1, 213. Smith adds that the "the second duty of the sovereign [is] protecting, as far as possible, every member of the society from the justice or oppression of every other member of it" (*Wealth of Nations*, Vol. II, Bk. V, Ch. 1, Pt. Two, 231). So, from Smith we get the important government objectives of national defense and law and order.

Chapter 9: Boosting Productivity

1 "BLS Productivity and Costs, Second Quarter 2022, Revised" News Release, Bureau of Labor and Statistics, September 1, 2022, https://www.bls.gov/news.release/ar-
chives/prod2_09012022.pdf.

2 Unit labor costs tell us the actual cost of each worker. An increase/decrease in productivity
will, all else equal decrease/increase unit labor costs. An increase/decrease in worker compensation will increase/decrease unit labor costs, all else equal.

3 An interesting and well-documented feedback occurs with increasing productivity: as labor
productivity increases, so do nominal wages, which enables workers to improve their
health and education since as we become wealthier, we demand more such goods. This, in
turn, increases labor quality and hence productivity in an upward cycle.

4 The term *stagflation* was coined by the British Conservative Party politician and government
minister, Iain Macleod, in a speech before the House of Commons in 1965. He called the
inflation and low growth strangling the British economy during the 1960s, a "stagflation
situation" ("What Is Stagflation, What Causes It, and Why Is It Bad?" Investopedia, July
31, 2022, https://www.investopedia.com/terms/s/stagflation.asp.).

5 The BLS excludes the public sector since government-provided goods are not sold in a market to individual buyers. Therefore, it is extremely difficult to estimate the economic value
of public sector output. Most productivity experts believe that productivity has grown less
rapidly in the public sector than in the private sector. For this reason, the BLS data tend to
overstate the entire economy's productivity growth" (McConnell et al., 2021, p. 457).

6 Of course, they can decrease for the same reasons.

7 A widely cited study found that during the period 1959-2006, 12 percent of US productivity
gains was due to increased worker education and training; 35 percent to increased efficiency of existing resources; and 53 percent to increases in the capital (Dale Jorgenson,
Mun S. Ho, and Kevin J. Stiroh, "A Retrospective Look at U.S. Productivity Growth Resurgence," Journal of Economic Perspectives, Winter 2008).

8 Typically, immediately after new innovations are implemented, output initially declines, given
the innovation's newness; then it increases slightly, followed by an upward explosion. It
takes time to learn the ropes, so to speak, to experiment, and to become accustomed to the
newness. But then, once the innovations bear fruit and the production factors acclimate,
productivity takes off abruptly.

9 Shawn Sprague, "The US Productivity Slowdown: An economy-wide and indus-try-level
analysis," Monthly Labor Review, April 2021, https://www.bls.gov/opub/mlr/2021/arti-
cle/the-us-productivity-slowdown-the-economy-wide-and-industry-level-analysis.htm.

10 Rhodes, *Energy: A Human History.*

11 "What Is Stagflation, What Causes It, and Why Is It Bad?" Investopedia, 2022. Although I
agree with *Investopedia* that the key to preventing stagflation (just like preventing inflation)
is "for economic policymakers to be extremely proactive in avoiding it."

Chapter 10: Simplifying the US Tax Code

1 Smith's 1776 book, *An Inquiry into the Nature and Wealth of Nations,* continues to be widely
read for an understanding of how markets work and how a market system can best provision
for all citizens. In his day, government intervention was quite extensive, especially in sus-
taining monopolies.

2 While many state and local taxes are also regressive, the focus of this chapter is on federal
taxes.

3 For a good discussion of the historical relationship between taxes and growth see Arthur Laffer,
Brian Domitrovic, and Jeanne Cairns Sinquefield, *Taxes Have Consequences: An Income Tax
History of the United States* (New York: Post Hill Press, 2022..

4 See "The Early Laffer Curve, 1974," The Laffer Center, https://laffercenter.org/docu-ments/the-early-laffer-curve-1974/, for a rendition of the Laffer curve just prior to its napkin appearance, as well as some interesting notes on the curve made by Laffer himself.

5 Although the ideas behind supply-side economics go back to Adam Smith (and even earlier), the term was coined by Herbert Stein, former economic advisor to Richard Nixon in 1976 and repeated later that year by the journalist Jude Wanniski.

6 For an interesting exposition of supply-side economics, and especially its genesis, see Brian Domitrovic, *Econoclasts: The Rebels who Sparked the Supply-Side Revolution and Restored American Prosperity* (Wilmington: Intercollegiate Studies Institute, 2014).

7 "About Supply-Side Economics," The Laffer Center, https://laffercenter.org/about/economics/.

8 "The 'Reagan Deficits,'" The Other Half of History, August 19, 2009, https://history-half.com/the-reagan-deficits/. The Other Half of History's fundamental objective is to redress the liberal bias in university education

9 Daniel J. Mitchell, "Tax Rates, Fairness, and Economic Growth: Lessons from the 1980s," The Heritage Foundation, October 15, 1991, https://www.heritage.org/taxes/report/tax-rates-fairness-and-economic-growth-lessons-the-1980s.

10 "About Supply-Side Economics." At the time it was the longest boom (simply defined as an economic expansion without a recession). But this record was replaced by a new record from June 2009 to February 2020. Indeed, three recessions occurred during this era: 1973-1975, 1980, and 1981-1982. While the latter occurred during Reagan's first year in office, its causal factors can be attributed to economic mismanagement under Jimmy Carter.

11 For a helpful and interesting discussion of tax brackets, see Julia Kagan, "Understanding Tax Brackets, With Examples and Their Pros and Cons," *Investopedia*, September 16, 2022, https://www.investopedia.com/terms/t/taxbracket.asp..

12 D'Angelo Gore, Eugene Kiely, Robert Farley, Lori Robertson, Brooks Jackson, and Brea Jones, "Trump's Final Numbers: Statistical indicators of President Trump's Four Years in Office," October 8, 2021, FactCheck.org (A Project of the Annenberg Public Policy Project), https://www.factcheck.org/2021/10/trumps-final-numbers/.

13 News Release, Bureau of Labor and Statistics, September 1, 2022, https://www.bls.gov/news.release/archives/prod2_09012022.pdf.

14 D'Angelo Gore, et al., "Trump's Final Numbers."

15 D'Angelo Gore, et al., "Trump's Final Numbers."

16 Peter Coy, "Trump Promised to Eliminate the National Debt in Eight Years: Good Luck with That," Bloomberg, March 9, 2017, https://www.bloomberg.com/news/articles/2017-03-09/trump-promised-to-eliminate-national-debt-in-eight-years-good-luck-with-that?leadSource=uverify%20wall.

17 D'Angelo Gore, et al., "Trump's Final Numbers."

18 D'Angelo Gore, et al., "Trump's Final Numbers."

19 Donica Phifer, "Trump Administration Considering Payroll Tax Cut as More Economists Express Recession Concern," Newsweek, August 19, 2019, https://www.newsweek.com/donald-trump-recession-payroll-tax-cut-1455127.

20 D'Angelo Gore, et al., "Trump's Final Numbers." In 2021, China's overall trade surplus was $458.9 billion, and since joining the World Trade Organization in 2001, its trade surplus has steadily increased ("China Trade Balance 1960-2022," Macrotrends, 2022, https://www.macrotrends.net/countries/CHN/china/trade-balance-deficit.).

21 Trump campaigned to significantly increase investment in infrastructure. However, his tax cuts were enacted first. Due to significantly increased budget deficits and the resultant congressional opposition, his investment policies were scrapped.

22 Jordain Carney, "McConnell hits brakes on 'phase four' coronavirus relief," *The Hill*, April 21, 2020, https://thehill.com/homenews/senate/494005-mcconnell-hits-brakes-on-phase-four-coronavirus-relief.

23 "Payroll Taxes" Peter G. Peterson Foundation.

Chapter 11: Americans Are Worse Off Under Biden

1 This sentence is, of course, from our Declaration of Independence.

2 Thomas Piketty, *Capital in the Twenty-First Century* (Cambridge and London: Belknap Press of Harvard University Press, 2017), 172.

3 Harvard's Lawrence Summers foresees unemployment rising to 7.5 percent and staying there until 2024, in order to reduce inflation to 1.6-3.2 percent (*Philip Aldrick, "Larry Summers Says US Needs 5% Jobless Rate for Five Years to Ease Inflation," Bloomberg, June 20, 2022, https://www.bloomberg.com/news/articles/2022-06-20/summers-says-us-needs-5-jobless-rate-for-five-years-to-ease-cpi?leadSource=uverify%20wall*). More generally, based on the results of a survey of ten US disinflationary periods since the 1950s, "a median fall in core inflation of two percentage points was achieved over a 30-month period only with a rise in unemployment of 3.6 percentage points, which corresponds to nearly six million Americans losing their jobs" (*The Economist,* October 8, 2022).

4 Ivanova, "Buckle up, America."

5 "Against expectations, Covid-19 retirees are returning to work," *The Economist*, September 15, 2022.

6 Collin Eaton and Jennifer Hiller, "As Gasoline Prices Drop, Electricity and Some Heating Costs Rise," *Wall Street Journal*, September 13, 2022, https://www.wsj.com/articles/as-gasoline-prices-drop-electricity-and-some-heating-costs-rise-11663096992?page=1.

7 Benoit Morenne, "US Gasoline Prices are Climbing Again, Pressuring Consumers," The Wall Street Journal, October 6, 2022, https://www.wsj.com/articles/u-s-gasoline-prices-are-climbing-again-and-may-get-worse-11665048601?mod=series_inflation.

8 "Winter Energy Outlook: Expect Soaring Energy Prices," Institute for Energy Re-search, September 20, 2022, https://www.instituteforenergyresearch.org/the-grid/winter-energy-outlook-expect-soaring-electricity-prices/

9 "Winter Energy Outlook."

10 Eaton and Hiller, "As Gasoline Prices Drop, Electricity and Some Heating Costs Rise."

11 Of the subgroups listed in the Census Report, American households with a bachelor's degree or higher did the best, seeing their incomes increase 2.7 percent from $112,393 to $115,456.

12 Paul Overberg and John McCormick, John, "U.S. Incomes Fail to Grow for Second Year in a Row, Census Figures Show, *Wall Street Journal*, September 13, 2022, https://www.wsj.com/articles/u-s-incomes-were-flat-last-year-census-figures-show-11663079099?page=1.

13 "State of Homelessness: 2022 Edition" National Alliance to End Homelessness, https://endhomelessness.org/homelessness-in-america/homelessness-statistics/state-of-homelessness/..

14 Victor Davis Hanson, "Is Biden's 'Success' Our Mess?" American Greatness, May 18, 2022, https://amgreatness.com/2022/05/18/is-bidens-success-our-mess/.

Chapter 12: National Security is Paramount, Beware of China

1 Robert B. Charles, "China Buying Global Food Supply?" AMAC, January 18, 2022, https://amac.us/china-buying-global-food-supply/.

2 Foreign investors (of which China is most preponderant) own 37.6 million acres of US farmland, or 2.9 percent of the total; a number, however, which has been increasing by 2.2 million acres per year since 2015 (Abbott 2022).

3 Charles, "China Buying Global Food Supply?"

4 Adam Minter, "One Reason for Rising Food Prices? Chinese Hoarding," Bloom-berg, January 4, 2022, https://www.bloomberg.com/opinion/articles/2022-01-05/one-reason-for-rising-food-prices-chinese-hoarding.

5 At the same it is quite troubling that the 30 percent of USA farmland is rented out by owners who serve as landlords and are not involved in farming. Case in point: "Bill Gates, has acquired over 260,000 making Bill Gates and his now divorced wife as the USA's largest private farmland owner" (Heilwell, 2021).

6 Betsy Joles and Cissy Zhou, "Farming out: China's overseas food security quest," Nikkei Asia, August 31, 2022, https://asia.nikkei.com/Spotlight/The-Big-Story/Farming-out-China-s-overseas-food-security-quest.

7 Fred Gale and Elizabeth Gooch, "Is China Buying Up Worldwide Agriculture Interests? USDA says Yes," Southeast Produce Weekly, April 26, 2018, https://southeastproduceweekly.com/2018/04/26/china-buying-worldwide-agriculture-interests-usda-says-yes/.

8 Elizabeth Anderson, "Why China Is More Prepared for Food Shortages than America," My Patriot Supply: Trusted Self-Reliance, October 6, 2022, https://mypatriotsupply.com/blogs/scout/why-china-is-more-prepared-for-food-shortages-than-america.

9 Charles, "China Buying Global Food Supply?"

10 Chuck Abbott, "Keep China out of US Agriculture, say House Lawmakers," July 5, 2022, Successful Farming, https://www.agriculture.com/news/business/keep-china-out-of-us-agriculture-say-house-lawmakers.

11 Minter, "One Reason for Rising Food Prices? Chinese Hoarding." China is motivated by haunting memories of widespread famines (due to its own political mismanagement) and its declining arable land and miserably low productivity. In addition, a devastating 2022 heat wave and drought has reduced China's agricultural production.

12 Lauren Richards, "China's Secret Police Are Illegally Operating in 25 Cities Across the World," Impakter, November 1, 2022, https://impakter.com/china-secret-police-are-illegally-operating-in-25-cities-across-the-world/#:~:text=What%20the%20world%20was%20unaware,monitor%2C%20threaten%20and%20terrorise%20Chinese.

13 Chad Bown and Yilin Wang, "China's recent trade moves create outsize problems for everyone else," Peterson Institute for International Economics, April 25, 2022, https://www.piie.com/blogs/realtime-economic-issues-watch/chinas-recent-trade-moves-create-outsize-problems-everyone.

14 Iowa Pork Producers Association, "Iowa Pork Facts, 2020," iowapork.org. Iowa Pork Producers Association, "20 Iowa Pork Facts," Oct. 12, 2022, https://www.southeastiowaunion.com/pork-producers/20-iowa-pork-facts/.

15 Bown and Wang, "China's recent trade moves create outsize problems for everyone else."

Chapter 13: Conclusion

[1] Edmund Burke, *Reflections on the Revolution in France,* (New York: Penguin Classics, 1968, originally published in 1790).

[2] Burke, *Reflections on the Revolution in France,* 163.

About the Author

Perry Johnson is the founder and owner of more than seventy companies that operate worldwide. These companies include Perry Johnson Registrars, Inc., and Perry Johnson Laboratory Accreditation, which do business in sixty-one countries around the world. Perry Johnson Registrars is currently the largest ISO 9001 Certification Body in the United States.

Mr. Johnson is considered a foremost authority in the field of quality and wrote what is considered the definitive book on ISO 9000: *ISO 9000: Meeting the International Standards* (McGraw-Hill, 1993), which is currently in its third edition. He is also the author of *Keeping Score: Strategies and Tactics for Winning the Quality War* (Harper Collins, 1989), *ISO 14000 Road Map to Registration* (McGraw-Hill, 1997), *ISO 14000: The Business Manager's Complete Guide to Environmental Management* (John Wiley & Sons, 1997), and the *ISO/QS-9000 Yearbook: 1998* (McGraw-Hill, 1998).

Mr. Johnson holds a degree in mathematics from the University of Illinois at Champagne-Urbana with a minor in economics and completed work in the graduate program for psychology at the University of Detroit. Now residing in Bloomfield Hills, Michigan, Mr. Johnson is married and has three sons. He serves as president for Perry Johnson International Holdings and a number of other companies. Outside of his daily responsibilities with his various businesses, Mr. Johnson is highly involved in the day-to-day lives of his children and is an avid golfer and bridge player. He has won not only five National Bridge Championships but has participated in the World Championships six times, with an eighth-place overall finish in the 1998 Championship in Lille, France.

As of the date of this publication PJR has certified more companies to ISO 9000 in the United States than any other registration body.